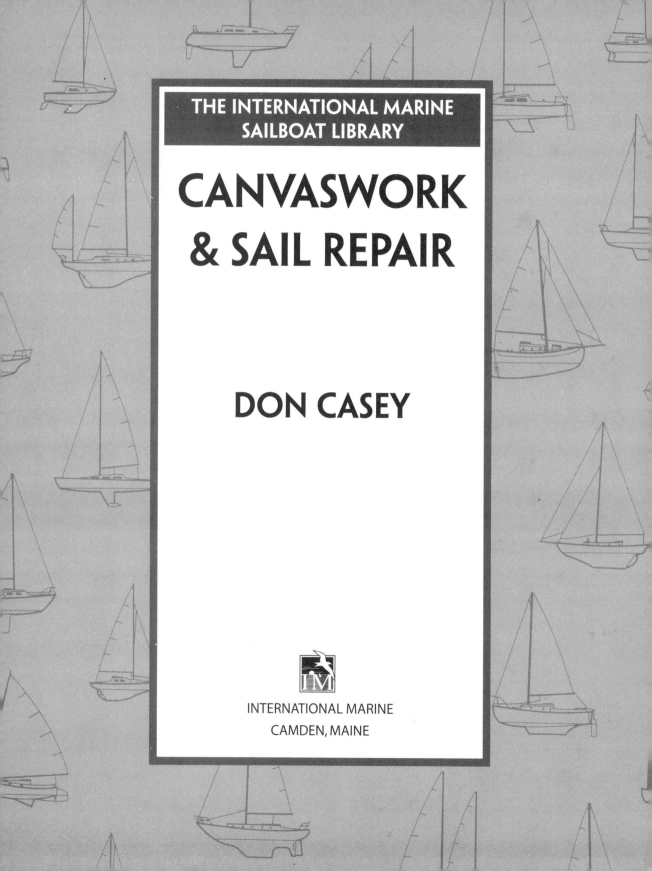

THE INTERNATIONAL MARINE
SAILBOAT LIBRARY

CANVASWORK
& SAIL REPAIR

DON CASEY

INTERNATIONAL MARINE

CAMDEN, MAINE

CONTENTS

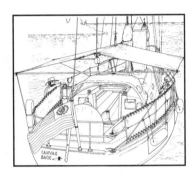

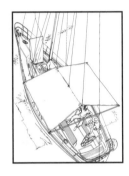

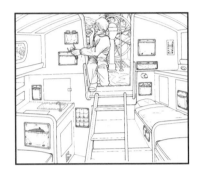

Introduction	**4**
What You Need	**6**

Sewing Machine Basics	8
Other Tools	10
Fabric	13
Other Supplies	16
Getting Your Machine to Sew	18
Diagnosing Problems	22

Flat-Sheet Projects	**24**

Fender Skirt	26
Lee Cloths	29
Weather Cloths	31
Flags	36
Windscoop	39
Harbor Awning	42

The Pocket	**50**

Hanging Storage Pockets	52
Zipper Pockets	55
Tool Rolls	56
Sheet Bags	58
Multi-Pocket Bags	60

The Bag	**62**

One-Piece Tote Bag	64
Hatch Cover	66
Two-Piece Duffel Bag	68
Winch Cover	70
Life-Jacket Box	72

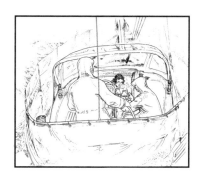

The Closed Box 74

Bolster 76

Zippered Duffel Bag 78

Cockpit Cushions 81

Settee Upholstery 86

Beveled Cushions 87

Bull-Nosed Cushions 89

Backrests 93

Custom Upholstery 95

Custom Canvas 96

Sailcovers 98

Boat Covers 102

Bimini Awning 106

Dodger 110

Sail Repair 116

Understanding Sail Shape 118

First Aid 119

Examining Your Sails 122

Restitching Seams 123

Patching a Tear 124

Replacing Panels 126

Batten Pocket Repairs 129

Chafe Protection 131

Clew Damage 132

Leech Lines 133

Hanks and Slides 135

Glossary 136

Index 138

Copyright Information 142

INTRODUCTION

The ozone layer—the BIG awning—is apparently getting threadbare. The amount of ultraviolet (UV) radiation passing through it and reaching the earth's surface is on the rise. These heavier doses of UV are destroying our Dacron sails, chalking our fiberglass decks, carbonizing our teak oil, and lifting our varnish. And they're giving some of us skin cancer at a rate that has doubled in the last two decades.

The long-term solution to the problems with the BIG awning is both complex and uncertain. The short-term solution is simple and efficacious: *Stay in the shade.* Of course, natural shade can be hard to come by out on the water. You can slap on a John Deere cap to protect your pate and your fine Roman nose, but that doesn't do anything for your sails or your varnish, which need the protection just as badly as that aquiline beak.

The most effective way to keep the sun off your boat and your body is with canvas covers and awnings. This isn't news; virtually every sailboat in your marina will be fitted with a canvas sailcover, and a substantial number will sport a fixed-frame awning known universally as a Bimini top. Sailcovers are standard equipment because they extend the life of expensive sails about tenfold. The popularity of the Bimini is no mystery if you've ever sailed a summer in the Torrid Zone.

But if a canvas cover adds life to your sail, wouldn't similar protection for other parts of your boat be a good idea? And if the patch of shade cast by a Bimini makes all the difference between *enduring* and *enjoying* a summer sail, couldn't the expansive shade of a good harbor awning be equally beneficial? The answers are yes and yes. Canvas's potential to protect your boat and enhance your enjoyment of it is practically limitless.

This book is about taking advantage of the myriad uses fabric has aboard a boat—all fabrics, not just canvas. Canvaswork, in marine usage, has come to describe anything aboard made of cloth. Sails, flags, ditty bags, and cushion covers are all canvaswork.

Why do your own canvaswork? Because you'll save a bunch of money. It's true that generic sailcovers and Bimini awnings aren't terribly expensive, but they rarely fit well either. If you want canvaswork to fit, it has to be custom tailored for your boat, and much of the essential canvas—interior upholstery, for example—is unavailable any other way. Canvaswork is not difficult, but it takes time. Every hour a sailmaker spends traveling, designing, measuring, sewing, fitting, adjusting, and installing adds dollars to the cost—lots of dollars—that you can eliminate by doing the job yourself.

A second reason for doing your own canvaswork is to get exactly what you want. Your sailmaker can keep fiddling with your project until it matches your vision, but with the meter running, that seldom happens. A week after your new weather cloths are installed, you say, "Gee, I wish I'd had her put in a pocket for a chart, and one for sun block," but fulfilling that wish is defeated by the cost or the hassle. However, if *you* made the weather cloths, by the next weekend they'd have pockets, probably at zero additional cost.

There is a third reason to do your own canvaswork: It is pleasurable. There is satisfaction in doing other jobs on the boat, but few of us will find much pleasure in barking our knuckles on the engine, grinding fiberglass, or sanding bottom paint. Canvaswork is different. It is clean, safe, and risk free; gratification is almost immediate; and you can generally work in a comfortable environment. Canvaswork can also be satisfying on a creative level, unlike changing the oil or bedding the stanchions.

The skills required to do stellar canvaswork are astonishingly few. The sewing machine does all the hard work. Your part is to cut the fabric to the required dimensions and guide the pieces through the machine. If a seam doesn't come out quite right, simply pull out the stitches and do it again. Try that with a carpentry project!

This book is designed to give you all the information you need to tackle virtually any canvaswork project you can conceive, but it takes a crawl-before-you-walk approach. Unless you are already comfortable machine-sewing heavy fabric, do not turn to page 86 and start reupholstering your boat's settee as a first project. Take the time to read at least the first two chapters and to make one or two of the items detailed in "Flat Sheet Projects."

"What You Need" is a canvaswork primer. Here you will find a description of the tools you need (including practical selection advice for those of you that don't already have a sewing machine). You will find information about all the most common marine fabrics. You will find out what size needle you need and what kind of thread works best. And you will learn how to set up a sewing machine and how to get it to stitch well.

"Flat-Sheet Projects" provides you with the opportunity to apply what you learned in the first chapter. All the projects are essentially flat sheets,

hardly more complex than a handkerchief—just bigger. These projects require hems at their edges; some require seams; and some require reinforcing, grommets, or other special features.

By the end of "Flat-Sheet Projects," you should have stitching, hemming, and seaming down pat. Subsequent chapters essentially detail canvas items a single step more complicated than those in the previous chapter. For example, in "The Pocket" we fold the flat sheet and seam two sides to form the basic envelope shape of the several illustrated projects. In "The Bag" we modify the envelope to make bag-like projects, and in the next chapter we put a lid on the bag to form the box-like structure of, for example, cushion covers. This evolution concludes with a chapter illustrating custom canvas items such as boat covers and dodgers—seemingly complicated projects, but by now you know better.

The final chapter is a bonus. Its initial focus is on emergency sail repairs—dealing with split seams and torn cloth—but once you have become comfortable sewing marine fabrics, there is little reason not to employ that skill to maintain your own sails. This chapter offers a number of sail-maintenance projects that will add years to sail life and save you money in the bargain.

In these pages you will find detailed instructions for more than two dozen projects, but they represent only a sampling of the useful items you can make for your boat with modest canvasworking skills. Don't be shy about modifying these projects or about striking out on your own. The possibilities are endless.

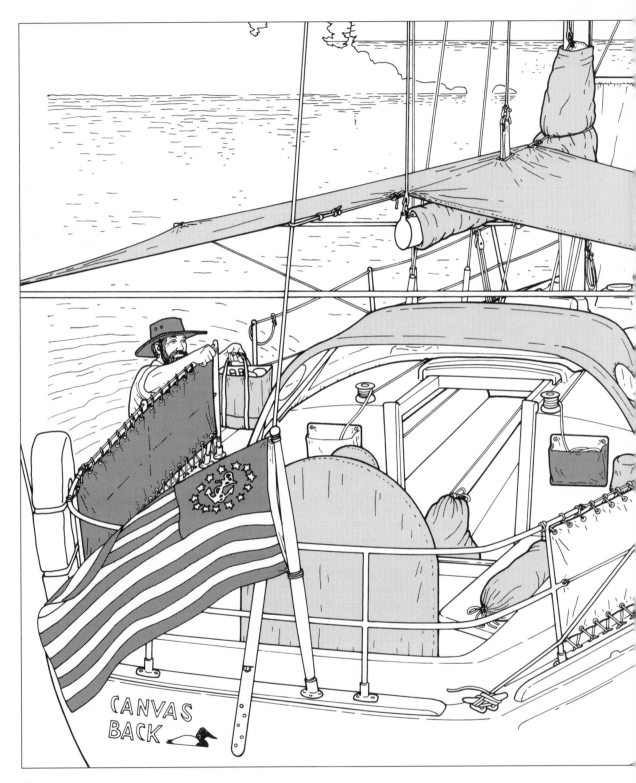

CANVAS
BACK

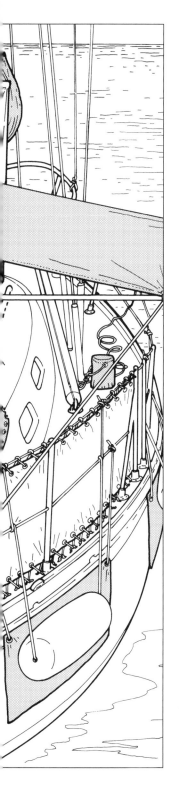

WHAT YOU NEED

Canvas has a long tradition on the water, equal in importance to wood and rope in the construction and operation of ships and boats for at least the last 2,500 years. Lashed to spars, canvas provided propulsion. Spread above deck, it provided respite from the elements. Tacked down and painted, canvas waterproofed decks. Spread between bulkheads, it cradled off-duty sailors. It continues to serve all those functions today, and more.

Despite this long history, many modern sailors tend to hold canvaswork at arm's length as a skill somehow beyond their grasp. This reluctance is especially surprising when you consider that an inexpertly fashioned canvas project doesn't put the boat at risk; the materials cost of even the most ambitious canvaswork project is likely to be less than an application of bottom paint; and for the time and money invested, canvas items offer the greatest benefit in appearance, convenience, or protection of virtually any boat improvement.

Learning to do your own canvaswork opens the door to scores of possibilities for inexpensively enhancing your boat and the pleasure of using it. Only a few simple skills are required to do journeyman canvaswork; anyone capable of sailing should have little difficulty mastering them.

Canvaswork projects are perfect for rainy days, the dead of winter, or the dog days of summer. The majority of a project (except for measuring and fitting) can be done indoors and away from the boat—at home, for example. You can complete an item in an uninterrupted effort or start and stop it over a period of weeks or months, whichever suits your temperament and the time available.

Like a trip around the buoys, you can probably get the job done quicker with the best equipment, but even an old boat is perfectly capable of completing the course. With not-for-profit canvaswork, completing the course is all that matters. Better tools may make a job easier or quicker, but they won't necessarily make it better. You need sharp scissors and a sewing machine that will make a decent stitch; beyond that, how good the finished item looks is up to you.

SEWING MACHINE BASICS

A lot of sailors own a swaging tool, a tension meter for the shrouds, or refriger-ation gauges, but relatively few think of a sewing machine as a boat tool. In fact, a good sewing machine is one of the most valuable tools a sailor can own, often paying for itself on the first project.

FEATURES AND ADJUSTMENTS

The shape of the head and the location of some of the dials may differ from ma-chine to machine, but most will have these basic features and adjustments:

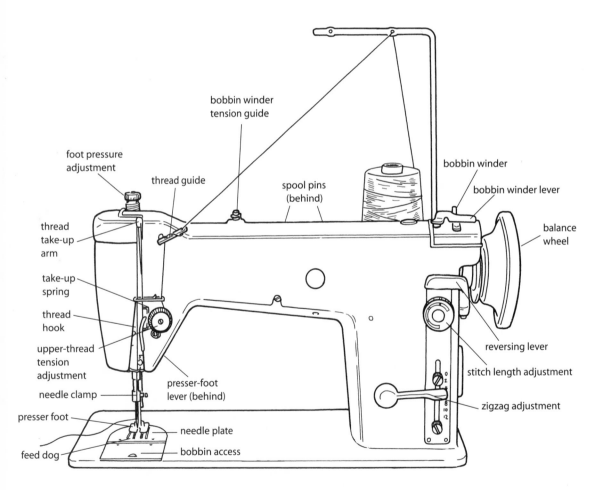

SELECTING A SEWING MACHINE FOR CANVASWORK

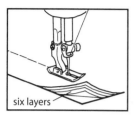

3 Look for a machine with vertical needle action. Bypass machines with slant needles.

walking presser foot

1 Take a piece of acrylic canvas with you. If you plan to do sail work, also take a piece of sailcloth. Make sure the machine will sew through at least six layers of your cloth. (When you hem two adjacent sides of a piece of canvas, you can have nine layers of cloth in the corner.)

six layers

4 Look for a long stitch. On most canvas projects, the longer the stitch, the better. You don't need a zigzag stitch for canvaswork, and heavy-duty straight-stitch machines can often be purchased very cheaply.

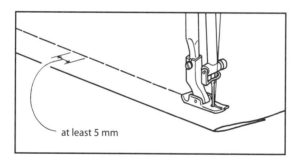

at least 5 mm

6 Adjustable foot pressure is mandatory. A machine with a "walking" presser foot will handle heavy materials better.

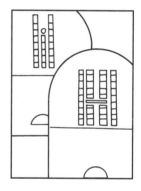

7 Interchangeable feed dogs are very useful, allowing the use of a wide feed dog on slippery fabric.

2 Look at commercial machine outlets and major repair facilities rather than domestic sewing centers. A domestic machine will do the job, but you want a heavy-duty one capable of a basic, solid interlocking stitch, not a machine that does buttonholes and embroidery.

5 If you anticipate significant sail repair or sail construction, a zigzag stitch becomes essential. A 6-millimeter width is adequate, but wider is better.

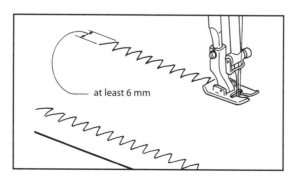

at least 6 mm

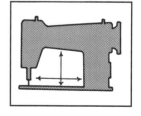

8 More underarm space is better.

OTHER TOOLS

Besides a capable sewing machine, the list of tools canvaswork requires is short. They are all inexpensive, so the difference in cost between a cheap tool and a quality one is only a few dollars. The quality tool will give better results and be less expensive in the long run.

FOR MARKING

A measuring tape, a *straight* yardstick, and a pencil are essential. A framing square can be useful. Use chalk to mark dark colors. Avoid pens and markers; ink will bleed through the material.

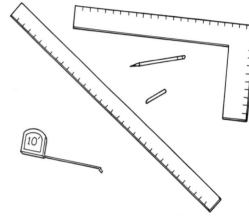

cutting tip

new scissors

seam ripper

FOR CUTTING

Start your canvaswork experience with a *new* pair of scissors. Lightweight vanadium-steel scissors (with brightly-colored plastic handles) cost under $10. Lefties—do yourselves a favor and get left-handed scissors. Nine-inch scissors are a convenient size. Also purchase a seam ripper. Cut sailcloth with a hotknife or a soldering iron.

FOR SEWING

Transfer tape looks like a narrow roll of brown-paper packing tape. When you apply it, then peel away the paper, only the adhesive remains. This lets you assemble two pieces or form a hem before you sew. Essential for sailcloth, it is also useful for canvaswork. You can accomplish much the same thing with a glue stick from an office supply store. You can also assemble pieces with heavy-duty straight pins.

If a project calls for a zipper or piping, you need a zipper foot for your sewing machine. Spare bobbins will minimize bobbin-winding interruptions.

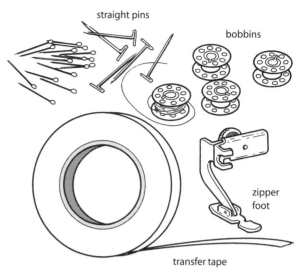

straight pins

bobbins

zipper foot

transfer tape

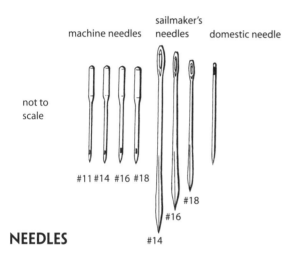

machine needles

sailmaker's needles

domestic needle

not to scale

#11 #14 #16 #18

#18

#16

#14

NEEDLES

Machine-needle sizes are logical—the larger the size, the larger the needle. Generally the heavier the fabric, the larger your needle should be. The smallest size you are likely to use is #12, the largest #22. A #18 needle is usually the best size for canvaswork, but if you have problems, try a larger needle. Needles should be designated "ball-point."

Just to confuse you, hand-sewing needle size decreases as the numbers increase. For handwork, a #16 sailmaker's needle is a good starting point.

FOR FINISHING

Durable grommet installation (spur grommets) requires a hole cutter and a good-quality die set. Except for the lightest-duty use, avoid the cheap die sets sold in washer grommet kits at hardware stores and marine outlets; you want a die set appropriate for spur grommets. You also need an installation tool for snap fasteners—about $5.

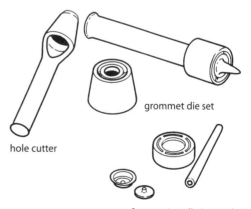

grommet die set

hole cutter

snap fastener installation tool

THREAD

You can stitch your canvaswork with variety-store thread, but it won't stand up to the sun and exposure. Unless you like restitching every year or two, it is sheer folly to use anything but polyester fiber thread, not spun polyester or wrapped polyester, or nylon. The kind of thread you need comes on a cone rather than a spool.

Virtually all lock-stitch machines require left lay (also called Z-twist) thread, so it has become standard; don't buy monofilament or thread that isn't twisted. "Bonded" polyester is preferable to "soft" finish. Thread designated V-92 is a good all-around weight, providing excellent strength and durability. For lighter fabrics and stitching that will not be exposed, V-69 can be a better choice. White is the only color you need.

1-ounce cone

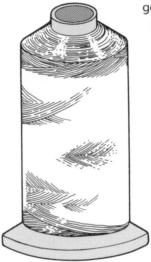

16-ounce cone

FABRIC

Choosing from among the endless array of patterns, colors, weaves, weights, and compositions of cloth available can seem daunting. For below-deck use, select any heavy-duty upholstery fabric in a pattern and color that complements the cabin. Just be sure the fabric is mildew- and stain-resistant, and that it isn't hot to sit or sleep on.

For exposed applications, choices are more limited. You will probably select acrylic canvas for most cover and awning applications, but you'll also find that natural canvas and a few other specialized fabrics are ideal for some marine uses.

ACRYLIC CANVAS

Most sailcovers are acrylic canvas. Once seemingly available only in blue, acrylic is today manufactured in a wide variety of colors and patterns. It is very UV-resistant, and most colors resist fading (red and some browns are the exceptions). Acrylic canvas "breathes" and is water-resistant, but it is susceptible to chafe damage. It is the best material for covers and a good choice for awnings. Common brands are Sunbrella, Acrylan, Diklon, and Sun Master.

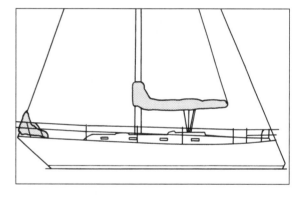

TREATED CANVAS

Natural canvas made of tightly woven cotton is a wonderful material, but its susceptibility to mildew and rot make it poorly suited to the marine environment. Treated canvas resists rot and mildew. Treated canvas is an excellent awning material, providing excellent UV-protection, and the natural fibers swell when wet to make the awning waterproof. Treated natural canvas is much less susceptible to chafe than acrylic canvas. Sunforger (Vivatex) and Terrasol are available in natural (off-white, called "colorless"), pearl (gray/green), and khaki; Permasol and Graniteville offer a variety of colors.

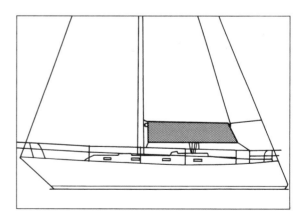

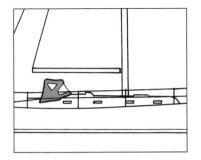

REINFORCED VINYL

Reinforced vinyl in the form of Naugahyde and similar fabrics was once the material of choice for almost all marine upholstery because it is waterproof. It is also hot in the summer, cold in the winter, sticks to bare skin, and promotes mildew because it doesn't breathe. Vinyl upholstery fabric remains the best choice for the exposed upholstery of powerboats, but has fewer advantages for sailboat use. Some vinyl-laminated polyester fabrics, such as Weblon, can be useful for Bimini awnings and dodgers.

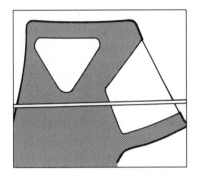

CLEAR VINYL

Clear vinyl is primarily used to put windows in dodgers and awnings. You can buy it by the yard, but if you want it to be water-clear, you will need to buy double-polished vinyl, sold in sheets (usually about 24 by 54 inches). For most uses, 0.020-inch thickness is the best choice—more flexible, easier to handle, and less expensive. Sheet clear vinyl is also available in 0.030-inch and 0.040-inch if added strength is necessary. Most clear vinyls cloud and darken with age; thick vinyls seem especially prone, perhaps because they are laminated from thinner material.

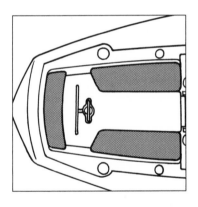

OPEN-WEAVE VINYL

Open-weave vinyl is woven polyester encased in polyvinyl chloride. Aside from marine uses, you have probably seen this fabric on lawn-furniture cushions and patio umbrellas. Open-weave vinyl is as waterproof as a screen door, but since it doesn't absorb or trap moisture, it is an ideal fabric for cockpit cushions, provided the enclosed foam is waterproof (closed cell). This fabric—Phifertex is perhaps the best-known brand—also makes good sheet bags and locker dividers. It is available in numerous colors and patterns. Machine-sewing open-weave fabric requires some special techniques.

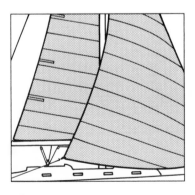

POLYESTER (DACRON)

Polyester fabric describes a lot of materials, including that awful double-knit in the leisure suit your brother-in-law still wears. For marine purposes, we are talking about sailcloth. Polyester, or Dacron, sailcloth is generally given a resin finish to help it hold its shape, but unfinished sailcloth is also available. Dacron makes great sails but poor covers and awnings. It quickly degrades in the sun, it is noisy in the wind, and UV radiation passes right through it, meaning it provides little protection from the sun. A subclass is vinyl-coated polyester fabric, such as Aqualon, popular for trailer-boat covers. This fabric has good abrasion resistance and color selection.

NYLON

Nylon cloth is used for light-air sails. It is commonly available in $^3/_4$-ounce (Stabilkote) and $1^1/_2$-ounce ("ripstop") weights. It is even less UV-resistant than Dacron, making it a poor choice for most canvaswork. Ripstop nylon can make a good light-air windscoop, but it creates an awful racket when the wind picks up. A soft, supple nylon cloth called oxford is available in 4- and 6-ounce weights. Nylon oxford cloth is often used for sailbags and similar items.

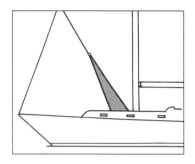

UPHOLSTERY FABRICS

There are hundreds of different upholstery fabrics, from silks and velvets to Herculons and Haitian cottons. Almost any upholstery fabric, in the right circumstances, can be used successfully in the cabin of a boat. Look for fabrics that are not excessively scratchy, hot, or subject to staining. Mildew resistance is a plus. For loose-cushion covers, washable fabrics will soon be appreciated. Buy a couple of yards of the cloth you are contemplating and sit on it, sleep on it, spill on it, and wash it (measure it first to check for shrinkage). If it passes all your tests AND you still like the pattern after a couple of weeks, it will likely be a good choice.

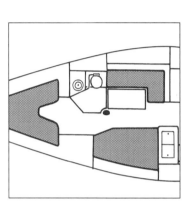

COLORS AND PATTERNS

COLORS AND PATTERNS ARE A MATTER OF TASTE, but there are some rules—guidelines really. Interior designers often rely on the color wheel to help in putting colors together. When the primary colors—red, yellow, and blue—are mixed, they form the secondary colors located between them on the wheel—orange, green, and violet. The warm colors (red, orange, yellow) are on the top half of the wheel; the cool colors (green, blue, violet) are at the bottom.

When you pick a color on the wheel, those on either side of it are *related* and will harmonize with it. The color opposite your selection is *complementary* and can be used success-fully as a contrasting color. The remaining colors are *discordant* and will have a jarring effect in combination. Select warm colors for a boat used in the often-dreary weather of the temperate zones; cool colors provide pleasant respite from the bright, hot tropics. The neutrals—white, black, gray, brown, and beige—aren't part of the color wheel (technically, they aren't colors) and can be used to good effect with any of the colors on the wheel. A color scheme should generally have an odd number of elements.

Patterns and textures add interest and make the cabin more "homey." But beware of excessively busy patterns; in a seaway, they can cause some people to feel queasy.

OTHER SUPPLIES

Most canvaswork projects require some method of attachment or closure, or both. Depending on the canvaswork project you take on, you will need some of the following hardware items. For bunk and settee cushions, you will also need an appropriate filler.

GROMMETS

Grommets provide a convenient means of tying awnings and covers in place. They can also provide additional ventilation. The grommets sold in most hardware stores and chandleries are washer grommets—adequate for only the lightest duty. For heavy-duty canvaswork you need spur grommets. If you fail to make the effort to obtain spur grommets, you are almost certain to regret that failing when the washer grommets pull out of the canvas. Spur grommets cost only pennies more than washer grommets; buy a one-gross box and you will cut the per-grommet cost and have enough grommets for a decade of personal projects. For general use, No. 2 grommets ($^3/_8$-inch hole) are usually a good size. Be sure your die set is for spur grommets.

spur grommet

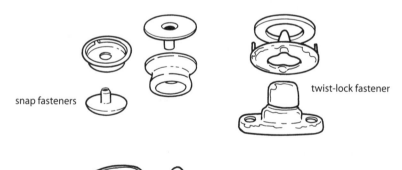

snap fasteners

twist-lock fastener

stud fastener (Lift-the-Dot)

SNAP FASTENERS

Snap fasteners are easy to install with an inexpensive installation tool. Be sure you buy good-quality snaps with bronze springs; cheap snap fasteners soon disintegrate in the marine environment. Stud fasteners (Lift-the-Dot) work similarly to snaps, but can be a better choice in some applications. Both snap and stud fasteners work better when the stress is mostly shear. Where the stress will be perpendicular to the fastener (lifting) a twist-lock fastener may be called for.

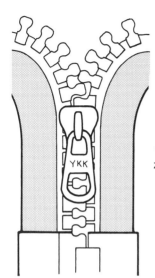

ZIPPERS

The easiest way to get the foam inside a cushion cover is through a zippered opening. Zippers are also useful for allowing a dodger window to be opened for ventilation, for extending a Bimini awning at anchor, and for allowing a cover to fit around a spar or other deck feature. Metal zippers have no place on a boat. Use only heavy-duty plastic zippers; the slide also *must* be plastic. The best are the YKK Delrin zippers. These come in two sizes—#5 and #10. The #10 zipper is larger and much stronger, and superior for almost any use imaginable aboard a boat. Select a #5 zipper only for light duty use or where a large zipper would be obtrusive.

VELCRO

Hook and loop tape (Velcro) has a number of uses aboard a boat, most notably as a secure way of attaching bug screens around hatches. It is also useful for holding cushions in place and for fastening covers and closing bags. Velcro is sometimes used to close cushion covers, but although it is cheaper than a zipper, it is also inferior for this purpose. Velcro is sold by the foot and is often available from discount suppliers. One inch is a good general-purpose width.

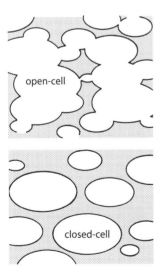

FOAM

Almost all cushions aboard boats are foam-filled. Open-cell foam (typically polyurethane) is the usual choice for settees and bunk cushions. If a cushion will be used for sleeping, adequate firmness is essential. Terms such as "Firm," "Extra Firm," etc., are meaningless. Select a foam that is compression-rated at at least 45 or 50 pounds (or with a density above 1.8 lb./cu. ft.). The best test is to try it; you may want 60- or 70-pound foam. Settee backs (not convertible to bunks) should be softer—try 30-pound. For cockpit cushions use only closed-cell foam (Airex or equivalent). Because closed-cell foam won't absorb water (open-cell foam is essentially a sponge), some sailors use it for all cushions, but closed-cell foam tends to compress rather than support. Sleeping on it may leave you with a backache, and when you roll over, your depression in the foam remains (for a while), making for a lumpy mattress. Buy 2-inch-thick closed-cell foam; 4 inches is a good thickness for open-cell foam.

open-cell

closed-cell

GETTING YOUR MACHINE TO SEW

Learning to run a sewing machine is not difficult, but spending an hour or two with someone with good machine-sewing skill can accelerate the process. Mostly you need to know how to thread the machine and how to set thread tension. After that, getting a tight, uniform stitch in a particular material is mostly trial and error. Sit down with some scrap cloth and see what effect differing adjustments have. There is no substitute for practice.

OIL THE MACHINE

To operate properly, all sewing machines require *regular* and *thorough* oiling. Before starting every project, tilt the machine back and brush the mechanism free of lint and thread. Then, using sewing-machine oil, apply the specified number of drops to every spot shown in the manual. If you don't have a manual for your machine, put two or three drops of oil in every drilled hole in the mechanism parts and in every hole in the base and the head. Oil sliding mechanisms, such as the needle bar, and both sides of every bushing (or bearing the shafts rotate in). Run the machine (without thread) to distribute the oil. Wipe off any excess, then run several rows of stitching on scrap material.

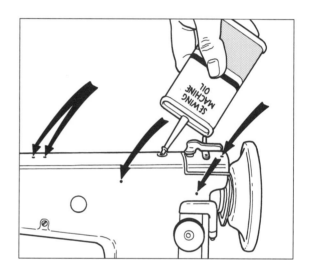

PULLING THREAD FROM A CONE

Spooled thread sits on a spool pin on the back side of the head, the spool rotating as the thread is pulled from it. But commercial-grade thread (long-strand polyester) comes on tubes or cones, and the thread must be pulled from the top. A length of coat hanger wire can easily be bent into a thread guide to feed commercial thread to your machine.

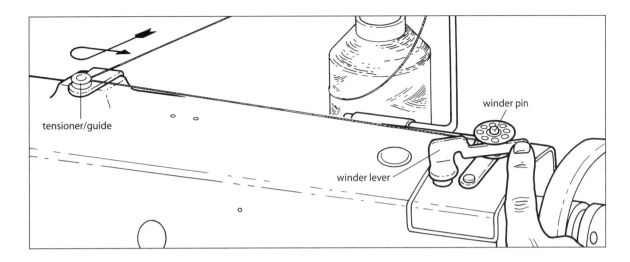

tensioner/guide

winder pin

winder lever

BOBBIN WINDING

Bobbin winders vary, but all operate in essentially the same way. Bring the thread from the cone through the tensioner/guide for the winder, and wrap several turns around an empty bobbin. (You will need fewer turns if you feed the end out through the hole in the bobbin's side.) Place the bobbin on the winder pin, paying attention to which way the pin rotates, then engage the drive wheel by pushing the winder lever. Running the machine winds the bobbin. Some machines have a knob on the balance wheel to release it so that the needle doesn't run when you are winding bobbins. The winder will automatically disengage when the bobbin is full.

THREADING THE MACHINE

Again, follow the instructions in your machine's manual. In general, pass the thread through the top thread guide, around the disks of the tensioner, over the take-up spring, under the thread hook, through the take-up arm, and down through the appropriate guides to the needle. The presser-foot lever must be up to release the tensioner disks. The top guide often has three holes for the thread to pass through (down-up-down), but passing the thread through the first hole, then looping it around the guide and down through the third hole sometimes helps prevent unwanted twist. Thread the needle from front to back or from left to right, depending on your machine. Pull out at least 6 inches of thread.

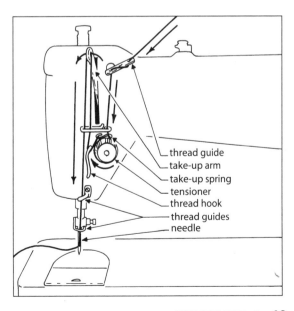

thread guide
take-up arm
take-up spring
tensioner
thread hook
thread guides
needle

BOBBIN TENSION

You adjust bobbin tension by tightening or loosening a tiny tension screw on the bobbin case. To remove the bobbin case from the machine, open the door in front of the needle plate—some slide, some lift. With the needle in the up position, grasp the bobbin-case latch lever and pull it, retrieving the case (and the bobbin). Release the lever and shake the bobbin out of the case. Drop in the fresh one, making sure it winds in the proper direction (usually clockwise from the open side of the case), and draw the end of the thread into the slit in the case and under the tension spring. The thread should pull smoothly but with resistance. If it pulls freely, tighten the tension screw slightly; if it pulls stiffly or unevenly, loosen the screw slightly. Leave several inches of thread hanging free and replace the bobbin case, snapping it in place. Pick up the bobbin thread by holding the top thread and rotating the balance wheel (top) away from you. When the needle returns to the top, pulling the top thread will bring up the bobbin thread.

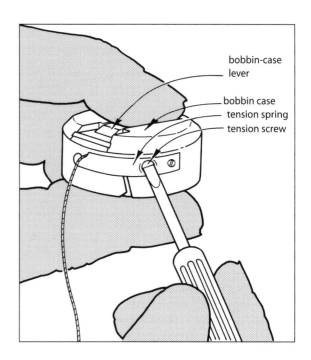

bobbin-case lever

bobbin case

tension spring

tension screw

STITCH LENGTH

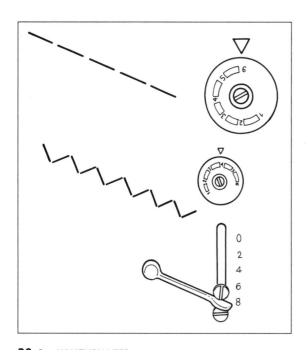

For almost all canvaswork, you want the longest stitch your machine is capable of sewing. Long stitches will minimize or eliminate needle puckers in acrylic canvas. Adjust the dial or lever to its maximum setting. The exception to this rule is sail seams, where you are using a zigzag stitch. In that instance you want square stitches—a 90-degree angle between stitches. The appropriate length will depend on how *wide* a stitch your machine can make.

FOOT PRESSURE

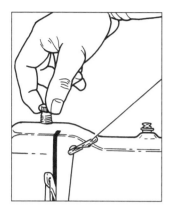

You don't need to adjust the foot pressure unless your machine feeds unevenly or skips stitches. In both cases, increasing the foot pressure may help. Some machines have only two settings—light and heavy. You want heavy— depress the button on top of the needle bar. Other machines have variable foot pressure that you adjust by turning a knurled knob at the top of the needle bar. Don't be afraid to crank it down if you're having problems.

UPPER-THREAD TENSION

After you get the machine set up for heavy material, you will normally need to make only upper-thread tension adjustments as you tackle canvas projects that vary in material and/or layers. The idea is to get the interlock between the two threads to be buried in the material. This is easy with soft fabric, more difficult with stiff acrylic canvas, and impossible with hard fabric like Dacron sailcloth. Sew a row of stitches through three layers of your fabric and examine them on both sides. If the bottom thread is straight, tighten the upper-thread tension. If the top thread is straight, loosen the upper-thread tension. If you have individual stitches on both sides, don't touch a thing. When you are unable to get the stitch you want, try adjusting the bobbin tension. Changing to a needle one size larger will also help.

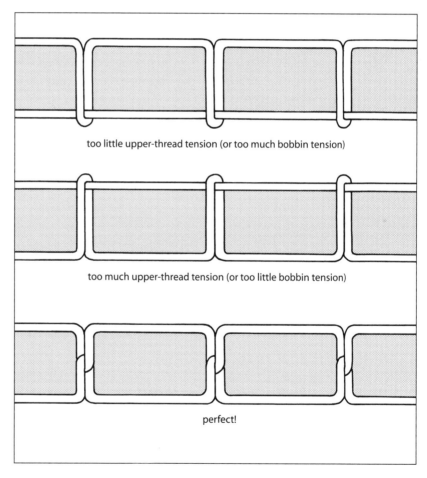

too little upper-thread tension (or too much bobbin tension)

too much upper-thread tension (or too little bobbin tension)

perfect!

DIAGNOSING PROBLEMS

You are likely to encounter some common problems. Here is a gallery of what they look like and how to cure them. Make all tension adjustments in small increments and run another test row of stitches.

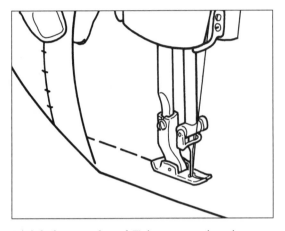

Straight bottom thread. Tighten upper-thread tension. Loosen bobbin tension. Change to larger needle.

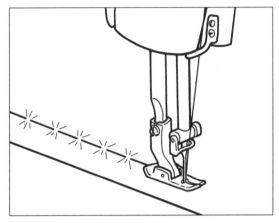

Puckered stitches. Increase stitch length. Change to smaller needle. Reduce *both* upper-thread tension and bobbin tension. Try lighter thread.

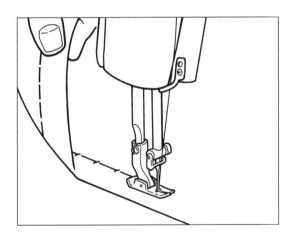

Straight top thread. Loosen upper-thread tension. Tighten bobbin tension. Make sure thread is feeding freely from tube or cone.

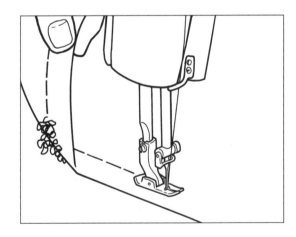

Bird's nest. Upper thread is not between tension disks. Presser foot is not down.

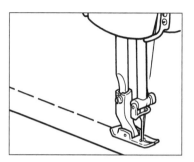

Broken thread. Loosen upper-thread tension. Make sure thread isn't jammed or snagged. Make sure needle is installed properly. Needle may be bent; install new needle. Try a larger needle.

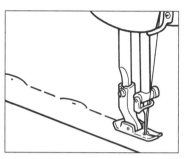

Skipped stitches. Increase presser-foot pressure. Change needle. Make sure fabric is feeding freely.

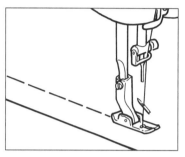

Broken needle. Make sure fabric feeds freely. Unjam top thread. Use a larger needle. Don't force too many layers under the foot. Apply less "helping" pull to cloth from backside of foot.

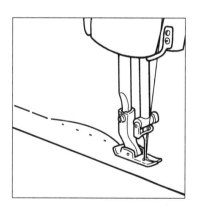

No stitch. Bobbin is empty. If bobbin isn't empty (i.e., broken lower thread), make sure bobbin spins freely in bobbin case. Clean bobbin shuttle and bobbin case, particularly under tension spring. Loosen bobbin tension.

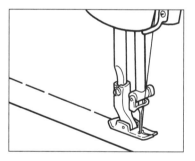

Uneven stitches. Make sure you are "feeding" the machine, not expecting it to pull the fabric. Raise feed dog (not all machines have feed-dog adjustment). Increase—or sometimes reduce—presser-foot pressure. Fit a roller presser foot. Replace worn feed dog. Help machine by pulling *lightly* on the fabric from behind the foot.

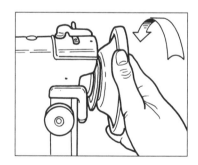

Machine doesn't run. No inertia; start the machine by turning the balance wheel by hand. Bobbin thread is jammed; work it free and clean out shuttle.

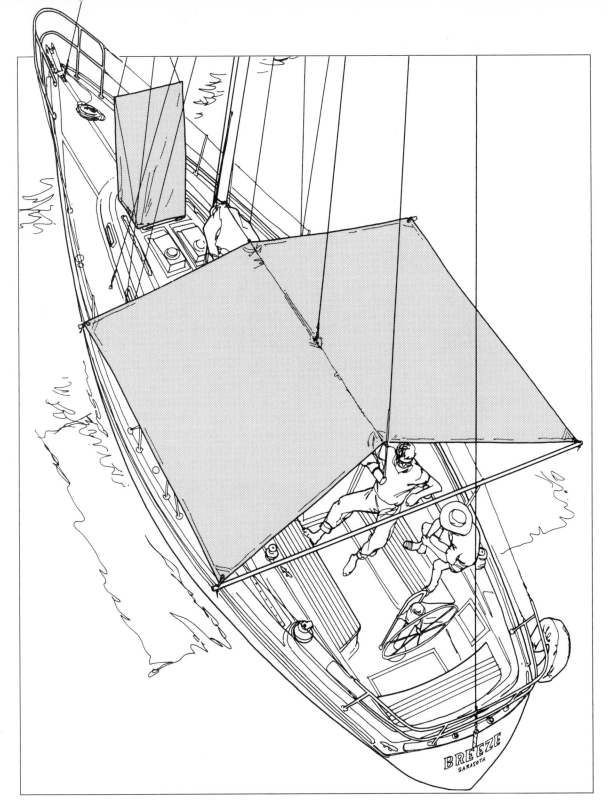

FLAT-SHEET PROJECTS

The first step toward becoming competent, even skillful, at doing your own canvaswork is to become comfortable with the sewing machine. Properly adjusted, the machine does all the work; you just feed it. There is little difference between stitching canvas on a sewing machine and making a scroll-cut in plywood on a bandsaw; you simply guide the material to keep the marked line at the front edge of the blade or, in this case, under the needle. To understand this better, draw a selection of spirals and geometric shapes on a piece of brown paper, then unthread your machine and "sew" the paper on the lines. This is also good practice for guiding the material.

Use some scrap fabric for your initial sewing efforts. Once you have mastered the coordination between guiding the material and applying the correct amount of pressure to the foot control for a comfortable sewing speed—and occasionally helping start the machine by hand-turning the balance wheel—it will be useful to do some experimental stitching. Start with a row of stitches through two layers of fabric. Tighten the upper-thread tension one hatch mark and make a second row of stitches. Tighten it another mark and sew. Number the rows and record the upper tension setting for each, along with the bobbin tension, thread size (and type), needle size, stitch length, presser foot, material type, and number of layers. After you have tried four or five tension settings on either side of your initial setting, do the same thing again, but this time changing bobbin-tension settings. (Record bobbin-tension settings by sketching the orientation of the tension screw in the bobbin case.) Now try different needles. Different stitch lengths. Different presser-foot and feed-dog sets. Do the same thing all over with three layers of fabric. Then with four. This structured sequence will help you find the best *initial* settings for each sewing job. Some adjustment may be required because of differences in fabric, thread, or even humidity, but developing a notebook of initial settings for various fabrics and thicknesses can be a big timesaver.

When you can make your machine sew an even stitch through three layers of canvas, with the interlock buried, you are ready to tackle your first canvaswork project. An astonishing number of useful canvas items for your boat are simply a flat sheet of cloth with the edges hemmed. These are the easiest canvas items to make and are thus ideal for building your skills.

FENDER SKIRT

Dresses for your fenders don't work. They make the fender a giant roller, capable of painting your hull with creosote as tides or waves roll it up and down a piling. A skirt doesn't have this problem. Hang it from the rail between the fender and the hull.

Begin this project with a rectangular piece of canvas about 40 inches by 30 inches. Adjust these dimensions to suit; height should be slightly less than your boat's minimum freeboard. Treated natural canvas will be easier on your hull and resist abrasion better than acrylic canvas, and it costs less.

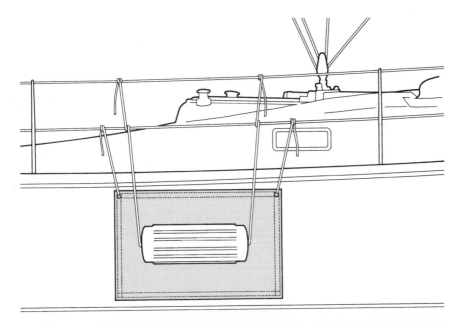

LOCKING STITCHES AT THE START AND FINISH

TO PREVENT STITCHES FROM PULLING OUT where the sewing starts or finishes, get in the habit of locking the first few stitches. If your machine has a reverse lever, sew about $3/4$ inch backwards, then release the lever and sew right over these stitches to lock them. At the finish, back-sew over the last $3/4$ inch of the stitching. If your machine won't sew backwards, lift the needle and foot after you sew about $3/4$ inch and reposition the fabric to the start of the stitching, then sew again right over the first stitches. Finish the same way.

SEWING A DOUBLE HEM

1 Fold in the sides (not the top and bottom) 2 inches and rub a crease into the canvas with the back of your scissors. Sew the fold down with a row of stitches $1/4$ inch in from the folded edge.

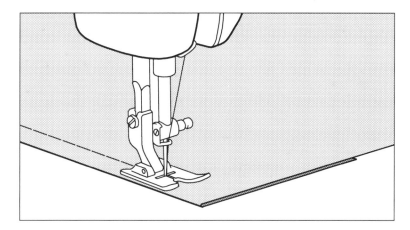

2 Turn $1/2$ inch of the raw edge under and rub it with your scissors. Run a row of stitches $1/4$ inch from this new fold. The result is a $1 1/2$-inch *double-rubbed* hem, or just a double hem. You will use this kind of hem *every* time you want a finished edge.

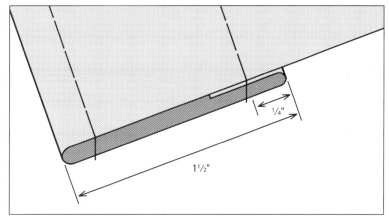

$1/4$"

$1 1/2$"

3 Hem the top and bottom edges the same way. Where the inner edges of the hems cross, you have *nine* layers of material! You may have to help your machine across these spots. Note that the finished dimension is 4 inches smaller than the cut size: *You must always allow extra material for hems and seams.*

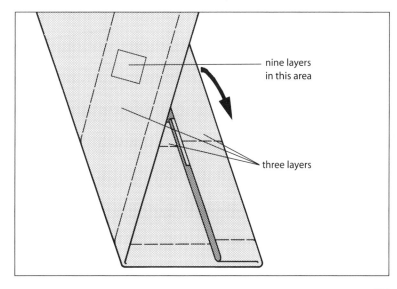

nine layers in this area

three layers

INSTALLING GROMMETS

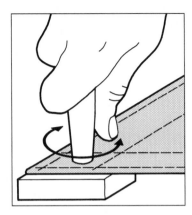

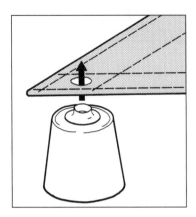

ANOTHER LAYER OF PROTECTION

FOR NORMAL USE a canvas skirt is more than adequate, but if your boat lies alongside most of the time, constantly riding against fenders, lining the inside of the canvas with terry cloth will be easier on your hull. Double hem the terry cloth at the bottom (not necessary if you are using a bath towel), then sew it to the canvas along the sides and top only, turning the edges of the terry cloth under.

1 With the cutter that accompanies the grommet die set, cut holes in the center of the squares formed by the overlapping hems at the two top corners. Back the cloth with a piece of wood. You will extend the life of the cutter by twisting it rather than hammering it.

2 For most common applications, including this one, use #2 *spur* grommets. Seat the male half of the grommet on the die and put the hole in the cloth over it.

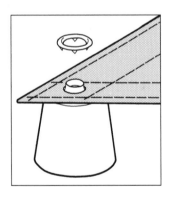

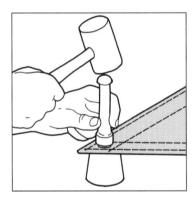

3 Fit the female half of the grommet—the ring—on top of the cloth over the protruding male half.

4 Insert the grommet setter, making sure the grommet is still seated on the die and that the setter is vertical. Tap the setter lightly to roll the edge and compress the two halves together. Finish with a harder blow to set the grommet. (If you are using a washer grommet, set it tightly enough that you can't twist it in the material.)

LEE CLOTHS

Lee cloths hold you securely in your bunk when the boat heels. The only construction difference between a fender skirt and a lee cloth is the addition of reinforcing webbing in the hem that gets fastened to the bunk—that and the choice of material. Lee cloths spend most of their lives stowed under the bunk cushion, so natural fibers are not a good choice. Dacron sailcloth is strong and has good moisture-shedding qualities, but acrylic canvas is also suitable and more comfortable against bare skin. If ventilation is a problem, use open-weave Phifertex.

MEASURING AND CUTTING

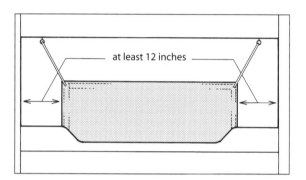

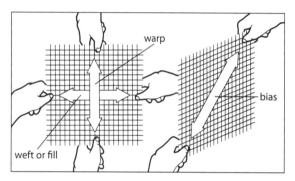

1 To allow for air circulation and to avoid claustrophobia, leave at least a foot open at both ends of a bunk: i.e., a 6$\frac{1}{2}$-foot bunk needs a 4$\frac{1}{2}$-foot (54-inch) lee cloth. For a finished height of about 18 inches, add 5 inches for the cushion thickness, 2 inches for screwing the cloth down, and 4 inches for hem allowance. Cut size is 58 (54 + 4) inches by 29 (18 + 5 + 2 + 4) inches.

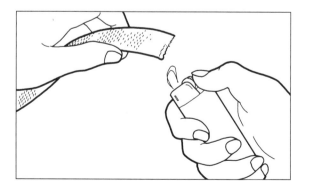

2 Woven cloth is stable along the *grain* of the fabric, i.e., parallel to the threads, but stretches and distorts when pulled *on the bias*—diagonal to the thread lines. Unless there is a specific reason to cut a piece on the bias, always lay out your pieces with the grain. Canvas generally has a "square" weave—yarns running lengthwise (warp) and those running across (weft or fill) are the same—so it makes little difference whether you align a part with the cloth edge or perpendicular to it.

3 Cutting with scissors is quicker and easier than using a hotknife. When a sailcloth item will be double hemmed, hotknifing isn't necessary. You need a piece of 1-inch webbing—Dacron or nylon—the finished length of your lee cloth. Cut the webbing with your hotknife, or play a lighter flame over the ends to fuse the threads (see the sidebar "Using a Hotknife" on page 125).

FABRICATING

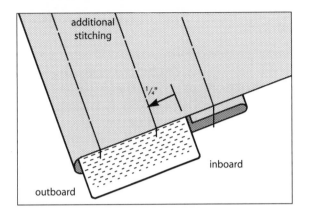

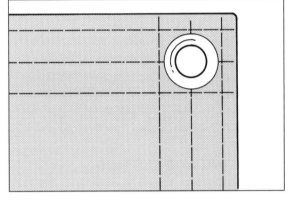

1 As illustrated on page 27, "Sewing a Double Hem," put a 1½-inch double-rubbed hem on all four sides of the lee cloth. Slip the webbing into the fold of the bottom hem before you sew it. Run an additional line of stitches ¼ inch outboard of the inboard edge of the webbing.

2 Install #2 spur grommets in the two top corners of the finished cloth.

INSTALLING

1 With the heated tip of an ice pick, melt mounting holes through the bottom edge of the lee cloth about 6 inches apart and centered in the webbing. Remove the bunk cushion and use stainless steel screws (# 8) and finishing washers to screw the webbing-reinforced edge of the cloth near the outboard edge of the bunk.

2 For light-duty use, the corners can be tied to overhead handrails, but for maximum security, through-bolt strapeyes or eyebolts to the overhead in appropriate locations. Tie lines to the grommets with bowlines or stopper knots, and make them long enough to allow the use of a trucker's hitch for plenty of purchase so the cloth can be pulled drum tight.

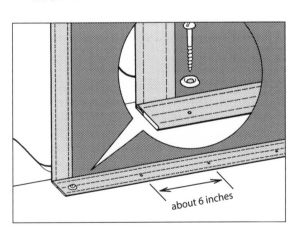

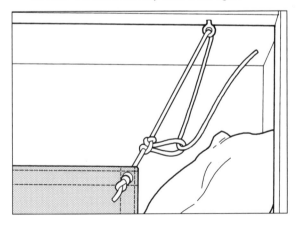

WEATHER CLOTHS

Also called spray dodgers, weather cloths provide protection from wind and spray, and they give a cockpit added privacy. Weather cloth construction is identical to a fender skirt except that the sides may not be parallel, and you may need a cutout for a line to pass through or for access to a cleat or block. Acrylic canvas is the fabric of choice.

1 Measure from the top lifeline to the deck, and from the stanchion on which the forward end laces to the one on which the aft end laces. The cloth can simply pass around intermediate stanchions. If you intend to lace the cloth to a curved rail, it will be easier to make the cloth straight and accommodate the curve with the lacing. A 2-inch hem allowance instead of 4 inches gives a finished dimension 1 inch smaller than the opening all around.

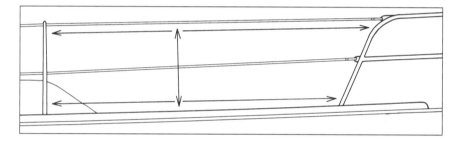

2 Sew a 1½-inch double-rubbed hem around the perimeter (see page 27 "Sewing a Double Hem.") For the best look, fold the hem onto the inside surface of the weather cloth; that means that opposing weather cloths are not identical, but rather mirror images.

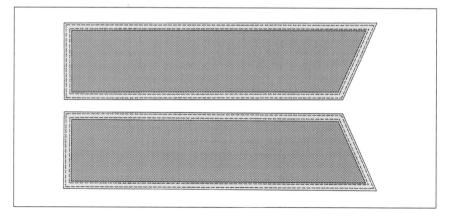

HEMMING CURVES AND CUTOUTS

1 Make the needed cutout after the cloth has been hemmed all around. In the following example, the cutout is a semicircle. The finished opening will be ¹/₂-inch larger than the cutout.

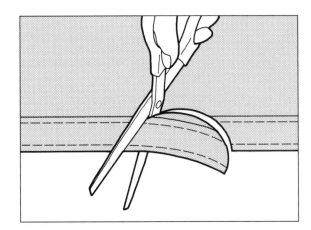

2 Cut a 2¹/₂-inch-wide arc of cloth matching the cutout on its inside edge. The legs of the arc should extend ¹/₂ inch beyond the hemmed edge of the weather cloth. (Use this same technique to put a curved hem on one end of the weather cloth to accommodate a curved stern railing.)

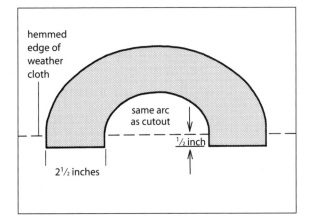

hemmed edge of weather cloth

same arc as cutout

¹/₂ inch

2¹/₂ inches

3 Place the arc on the outside (hems are on the inside) of the weather cloth, lined up with the cutout and extending ¹/₂ inch beyond the edge on either side. Sew the arc in this position with a row of stitches ¹/₂ inch from the inside edge.

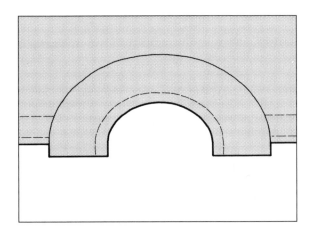

4 With your scissors, snip through the raw edges of both pieces, making a cut perpendicular to and about $\frac{1}{8}$ inch shy of the stitching. Repeat this every $\frac{1}{2}$ inch (every inch for larger radii) all along the curve, being very careful not to cut closer to the stitching than $\frac{1}{8}$ inch.

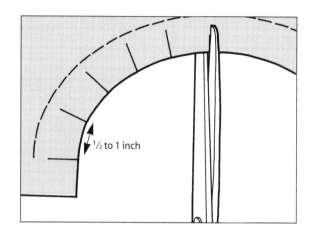

½ to 1 inch

5 The slits allow the concave edge to expand, so you can fold the arc from the outside of the weather cloth to the inside. Turn under the raw edges of the legs of the arc and run a row of stitches following the contour and about $\frac{1}{2}$ inch from the edge.

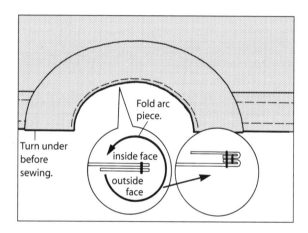

Fold arc piece.

Turn under before sewing.

inside face

outside face

6 Fold under and sew down the outside edge of the arc piece. In soft fabric you can deal with the excess fabric that results by sewing in evenly spaced darts—triangular pleats—but on stiff canvas it is better to remove this extra fabric by V-cutting the hem of a convex edge before folding it under.

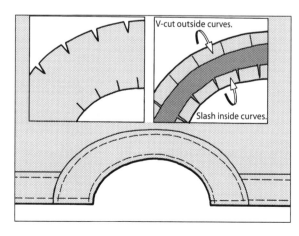

V-cut outside curves.

Slash inside curves.

INSTALLING WEATHER CLOTHS

1 Install #2 spur grommets at each corner and evenly spaced 6 to 8 inches all around the perimeter.

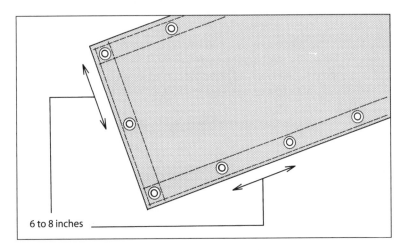

6 to 8 inches

2 Tie the cloth in place with short lengths of light line at the corners. Install small strap eyes on the deck, centered between each pair of grommets in the bottom edge.

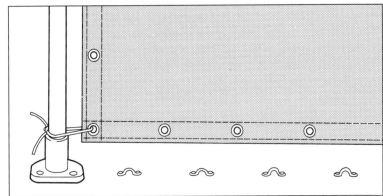

3 Use a continuous length of $^3/_{16}$-inch Dacron line to lace the cloth in place. The line will move and wear less if you throw in a half hitch every time the line passes over the lifeline, around a stanchion, or through an eye.

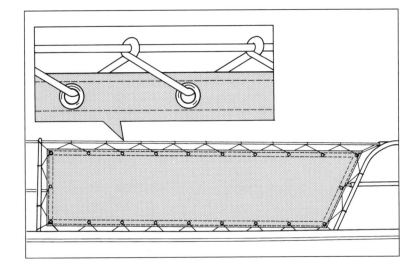

APPLIQUÉ—PUTTING LETTERS ON YOUR WEATHER CLOTHS

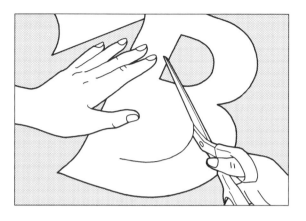

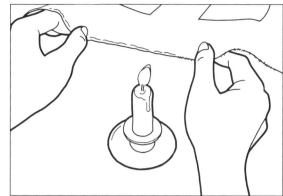

1 Cut letters from a contrasting fabric. If you want them to last as long as acrylic weather cloths, use acrylic canvas for the letters also.

2 Seal the raw edges of acrylic canvas by passing them quickly through a flame. Practice this skill first on scrap material.

3 Position the letters on the cloth the way you want them, then attach them with an office-supply glue stick. It is a good idea to rig the weather cloth and view the lettering actually on the boat before you sew it in place permanently.

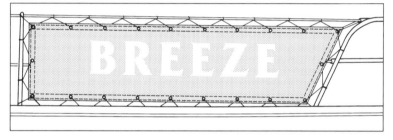

4 Set the zigzag width to about 4 millimeters (6 mm is the typical maximum setting), dial the stitch length down to about 3 mm, and adjust the tension. *Overcast* the edges of the letters; that is, sew around their perimeters with one side of the stitch just off the edge of the letter. Don't forget the inside edges of closed letters.

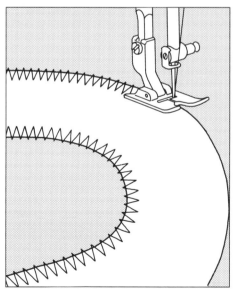

POCKETS

POCKETS SEWN to the inside of weather cloths can be very handy for holding charts, sunglasses, lotion, and innumerable other items. Instructions for fabricating patch pockets are included in the next chapter, "The Pocket."

FLAGS

Signal flags were once essential aboard boats for communication. Today their uses are more ceremonial, but a few flags can be required equipment. Most flags are easy to make. For flags that will be bright, durable, and fly well, select 4-ounce oxford nylon. The most common size is 12 by 18 inches, but 24-inch flags are a better fit for boats larger than about 35 feet.

Q FLAG

A vessel entering a foreign country is required to fly the Q flag, indicating that it is under quarantine until officials issue clearance. The Q flag is solid yellow.

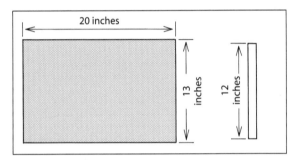

20 inches

13 inches

12 inches

Fold once.

Fold again, then sew both edges of hem.

½ inch

1 Cut the cloth an inch wider and 2 inches longer than the desired finished size: for a 12- by 18-inch flag, cut the cloth 13 by 20 inches. Cut a 12-inch length of 1-inch webbing.

2 Center the webbing on one short side, overlapping the cloth ½ inch. Stitch down the center of the overlap. Using the edges of the webbing as guides, fold the cloth over, then fold it over again. Stitch ¼ inch from the inboard and outboard edges of the hem.

3 Starting with the opposite short side, put a ¼-inch double-rubbed hem on the remaining three sides. Fold ¼ inch of cloth under, then fold it again another ¼ inch and sew it down with two rows of stitches. For your initial tries at this, gluing the hem down first with transfer tape or a glue stick may give you better results.

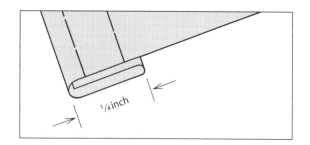

¼ inch

4 Put two #2 spur grommets near the ends of the reinforced edge.

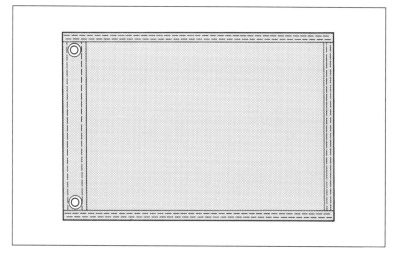

FLAT-FELLED SEAMS

WHEN BOTH SIDES OF THE FABRIC will be visible, join pieces with a *flat-felled seam*. The most secure method is to overlap the two pieces ½ inch and stitch down the center of the overlap. Fold the top piece of fabric under at the raw edge of the overlap, then flip the other piece over to enfold the other raw edge. This is a good place to use transfer tape to hold the fabric in position for sewing. Stitch near both edges of the seam to hold it flat.

This method has the advantage of having an internal row of stitches entirely protected from the sun, so when the exposed stitching begins to fail, the item will not fall apart.

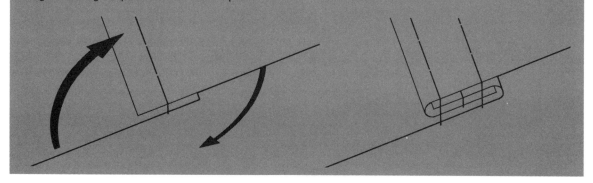

DIVER'S FLAG

Anytime a diver is in the water, the law requires the display of a diver's flag. Fly this flag from the spreader when you are near the boat, or attach it to a float-mounted pole tethered to you.

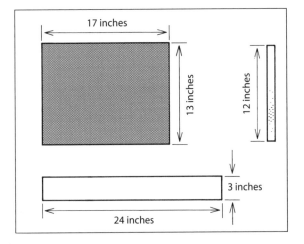

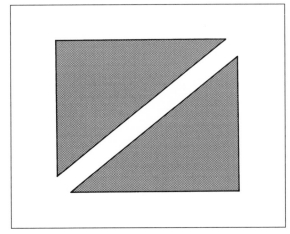

1 For a 12- by 18-inch flag, cut the red material 13 by 17 inches. You also need a strip of white material 3 inches wide and a couple of inches longer than the diagonal distance across the red—in this case, make the strip 24 inches long.

2 Draw a straight diagonal line between opposite corners of the red fabric and cut the piece in half on this line.

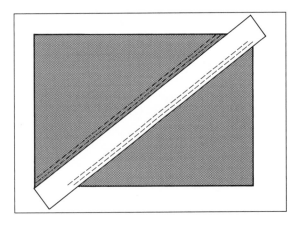

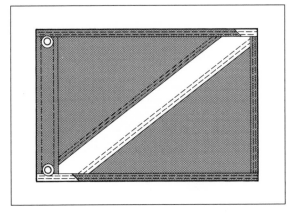

3 Sew the white strip to one of the diagonal edges with a ½-inch flat-felled seam (see page 37). Seam the other diagonal edge to the opposite side of the strip, aligning them as shown for the *flat-felled seam*.

4 Trim away the extra white material and finish the edges of the flag exactly like the Q flag on page 36.

WINDLESS DAYS YIELD the best diving conditions, but also the best conditions for powerboating. When it is calm is when you most want your dive flag visible, but instead it hangs straight down in a narrow strip of red. The solution is a diagonal batten. A wooden dowel will work, but a fiberglass sail batten is better.

Cut a strip of white fabric as long as the diagonal stripe in your flag and about 2 inches wider than the batten. Turn the edges under $\frac{1}{2}$ inch and sew the strip down on three sides on top of the white stripe. Slip the batten into the pocket to mark the length, then cut the batten to size and smooth the ends.

Insert the sized batten into the pocket and stitch the fourth side closed. Folding a piece of leather or canvas over the ends before you insert the batten will reduce internal chafe. Fly the flag with the batten at the bottom of the hoist end.

WINDSCOOP

There are lots of windscoop designs, but this one has the advantage of being simple and big, the latter especially important on hot days when the wind is lethargic. The disadvantage is that the boat needs to more or less face the wind, a problem in current or at the dock.

Treated canvas is a good material choice because it is quiet and chafe-resistant, but you can't put it away wet. Acrylic canvas requires less care, but you will need chafe patches where it touches the open hatch. Stay away from spinnaker cloth: the ability to "fill" easily is not a benefit with this design, and the crackle of the nylon when the bow gets off the wind will drive you crazy.

1 Open the forward hatch to about 45 degrees and make a paper pattern of a three-sided box that lies flat against the hatch and sits on the deck. You are only interested in the bottom edge of this pattern.

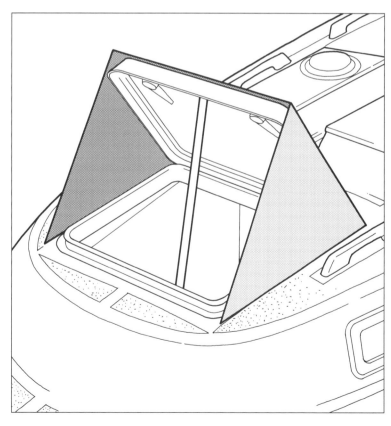

2 You can make this scoop as wide as you want, but a good rule of thumb is to make it about 2¹/₂ times the width of the hatch. The height is limited only by the diagonal distance to the headstay, but as a practical matter you will get ample height from two panels of 46-inch material, which will require only a single seam. For a 20-inch hatch, hem two 50-inch lengths of fabric side to side. Because you are joining finished edges (*selvages*), sew the pieces together with a simple ¹/₂-inch overlap seam. Overcast the edges with a zigzag stitch if you like.

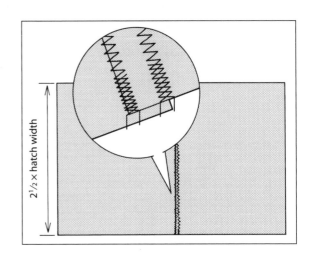

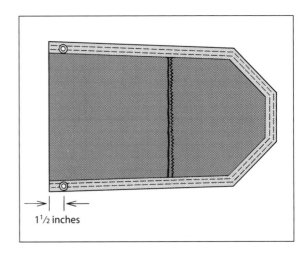

3 Center the bottom of the paper pattern along one of the short sides and trace its two angular edges onto the canvas. If you used the 2¹/₂-times rule, the pattern should fall an inch or two short of the edges of the cloth panel. If you made your scoop wider, extend the pattern line about 2 inches on either side, then connect it with a straight line to the top corners of the scoop. Cut on the lines.

4 Put a 1¹/₂-inch double-rubbed hem (see page 27) on all edges except the top. Install #2 spur grommets in the two side hems 1¹/₂ inches from the raw edge.

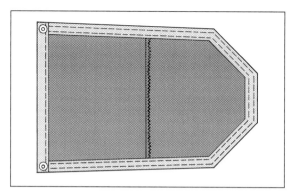

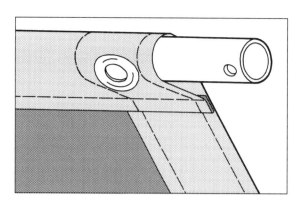

5 Finish the top edge with a 1½-inch double-rubbed hem, but omit the outboard row of stitches. This provides the pocket for the spreader.

6 Cut a length of aluminum tubing or metal electrical conduit (EMT) to the finished width of the scoop and slide it into the pocket. Mark it with the location of the grommets. Remove it and drill ⅜-inch holes in the conduit slightly outboard of the marks; this way the hoist lines will also prevent the canvas from bunching on the spreader. Sand the edges of the holes.

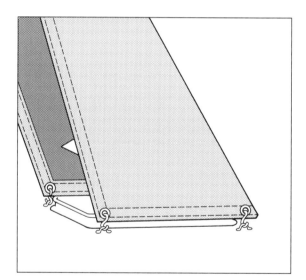

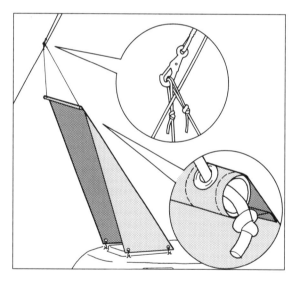

7 Install grommets at the four corners of the bottom edge, then install small strap eyes on deck at the locations of these grommets. S-hooks closed around the grommets expedite installation. Note that the hatch can be closed without removing the scoop.

8 Put stopper knots on the ends of two lengths of ¼-inch Dacron line and thread them from inside the spreader out through the grommet. Tie bowlines in the other ends of the lines and hoist them forward of the headstay. Some experimentation will be required to find the right length, but the taut lines should be in the same plane as the top of the scoop.

HARBOR AWNING

Perhaps you're wondering if an awning isn't too far advanced for an entry foray into canvaswork. Shouldn't awnings come later in the book? No. A harbor awning, in a typical manifestation, is nothing more than a bigger panel of canvas, hemmed all around, with grommets on the corners, and perhaps with the addition of corner reinforcements and spreader pockets.

The best material for a harbor awning is treated canvas in the natural off-white color. The natural fibers of treated canvas stand up well to handling, and harbor awnings given intermittent use can easily last 15 or 20 years. Natural fibers also swell when wet, making the fabric genuinely waterproof. Acrylic canvas depends on a coating to make it waterproof, and the proofing soon wears off awnings that are often folded and handled. Avoid dark colors, especially for tropical use; the radiated heat from a dark awning can be nauseating.

AWNING DESIGN

1 A flat awning has internal battens to spread it. It can be the easiest type to put up, but the most awkward to stow. It handles sudden windstorms well, and it can be inclined toward the sunny side for later shade.

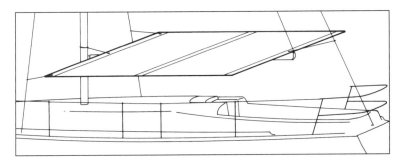

2 A tent awning is the easiest to construct and the easiest to stow. It is typically stretched between the mainmast and the backstay or the mizzenmast, with the four corners tied down to the shrouds, the lifelines, or both.

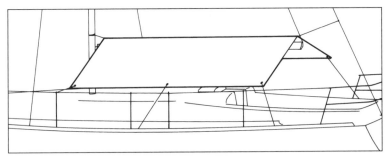

3 A pole awning is a tent awning with external spreaders. The spreaders allow the awning to be set higher for standing room and to extend beyond the rail for longer-lasting shade. The awning and spreaders are stowed separately.

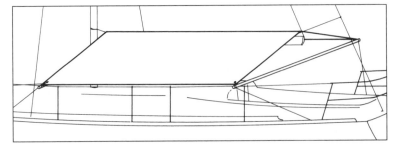

MEASURING FOR YOUR AWNING

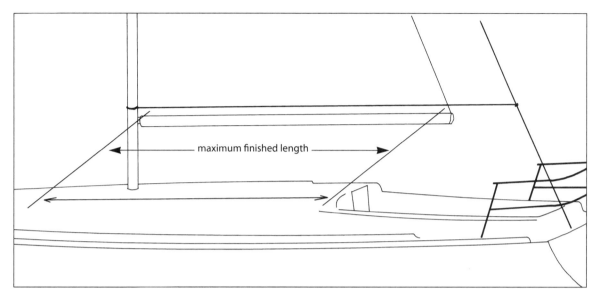

maximum finished length

1 Tie a line between the mast and the backstay (or mizzen). The maximum finished length of your awning is the length of this line between the mast and the topping lift less an allowance for tensioning.

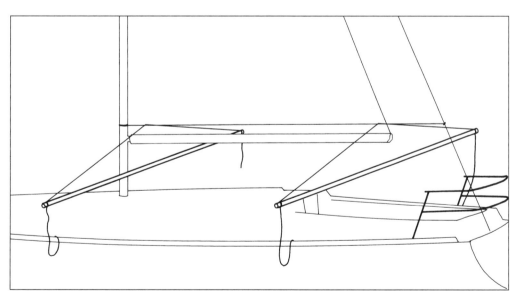

2 Tie lines from the ridgeline to your planned corner tie-off points. If you are making a flat awning, these lines must run straight across the ridgeline; if you are making a tent or pole awning, the lines will form an apex over the ridgeline. If you plan to use spreaders, simulate them now with reaching poles, boathooks, or what have you.

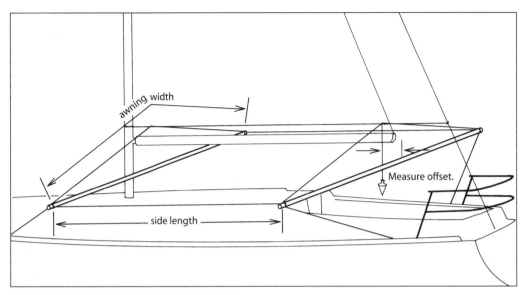

3 Tie fore-and-aft lines between the tie-off points. These simulate the sides of the awning, which will essentially be straight. If there is any rigging inside of these lines, you will have to make the awning smaller or install a zipper (see page 77) to allow the awning to fit around it.

These lines also let you observe the limits of the shade as the day progresses. The distance between the corner tie-offs, measured over the ridgeline, gives the widths of your awning forward and aft.

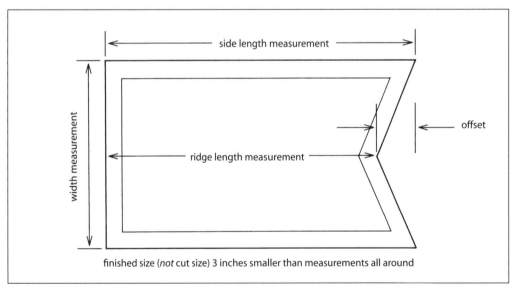

finished size (*not* cut size) 3 inches smaller than measurements all around

4 If your awning isn't a rectangle, measure the fore-and-aft distance to the mast or topping lift from a straight line between the tie-offs so you can duplicate the shape when you cut the material. Put all your measurements on a sketch of the awning. Now reduce the length and width by 6 inches: you need at least 3 inches of space at each tie-off point to allow tensioning, and you want the pull at the corners to be diagonal.

MAKING THE PANEL

1 Seams should always run athwartship on an awning so rain runs along, not under, them. Cut the canvas with a 4-inch hem allowance, plus an additional 3 inches for tent or pole awnings. If the awning width isn't uniform, be sure each panel is long enough for its location. Sew the panels together with a 1-inch overlap seam, sewing down the middle of the overlap with your widest zigzag stitch (with the stitch length adjusted to give a square stitch). Overcast both edges with additional rows of zigzag stitching—this is identical to triple-stitched seams on a sail.

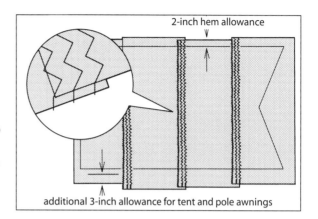

2-inch hem allowance

additional 3-inch allowance for tent and pole awnings

2 Straighten up the sides using scissors. If you allowed the extra 3 inches, cut a 3-inch-wide strip from one edge and set it aside. The length of the assembled panel, like the width, should be 4 inches longer than the finished size.

3 Cut a slight hollow into the side edges—about 1 inch for every 6 feet of length. This keeps the edge from flapping, just like leech hollow does in a sail.

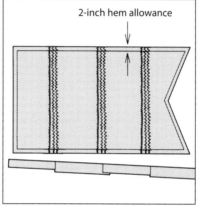

2-inch hem allowance

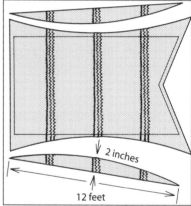

2 inches

12 feet

4 Sew reinforcement patches to the unhemmed panel. Add two layers of cloth at the corners, in the middle of the front and back edges (and the side edges if your awning will be fastened there), and at lift points in the center. Don't install lift patches now if the awning will have a ridge rope. For each reinforcement location, cut two patches to match the grain of the panel, one about 4 inches and the other about 6 inches on a side or in diameter. Align the large patch 2 inches from the edge and sew down the turned-under diagonal edge or curved edge. Slip the small patch under the large one and stitch $1/4$ inch inside its diagonal or curved edge. Make lift patches oval or diamond shaped, also with the top patch hemmed.

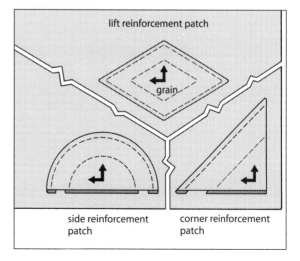

lift reinforcement patch

grain

side reinforcement patch

corner reinforcement patch

FROM PANEL TO AWNING

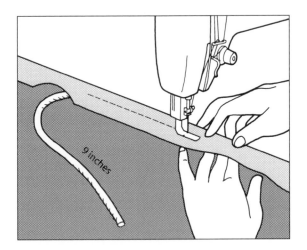

1 Roping the edge doubles or triples an awning's life and quiets the edges. Use $^3/_8$-inch three-strand Dacron line. Trim and hem the corners for a mitered hem (see below). Put the zipper foot on your machine with the needle on the right side. Starting about one-third of the way across one end of the awning, fold the edge over 2 inches, slide the rope into the fold, and stitch up against it. Leave 9 inches of rope free and keep the rope straight and taut as you sew. If the zipper foot is long, corners may be troublesome: do the best you can.

2 Rope the awning continuously all the way around, stopping about a foot short of where you started. Join the ends with a short splice, cutting half the yarns out of each strand to maintain the rope's diameter. Sew down the remaining section to enclose the splice. Now turn the raw edge under $^1/_2$ inch and sew it down all around.

3 If you elect not to rope the awning, put a normal $1^1/_2$-inch double-rubbed hem in it all around, mitering the corners. Whether you hem or rope, your stitching should catch the unsewn edges of the reinforcing patches.

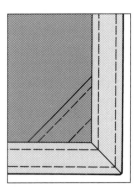

MITERING A HEMMED CORNER

YOU CAN REDUCE the bulk of hemmed corners by mitering them. Fold both edges over the normal hem amount and rub them to crease the material. Unfold them and cut the corner off diagonally $^1/_2$ inch from the intersection of the creases. Put a $^1/_4$-inch double-rubbed hem (see page 27) in this diagonal edge. Now put your regular double-rubbed hem in the sides. This way you need only to sew through six layers of cloth, instead of nine, and you get a flatter corner.

$^1/_2$ inch from the intersection of the creases

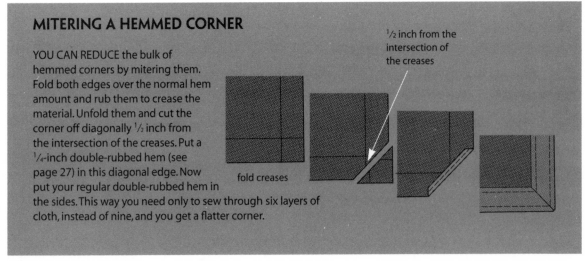

fold creases

4 Flat awnings require batten pockets at the ends and sometimes in the middle. Cut strips of canvas about 1 inch wider than 3 times the diameter of your battens and just shorter than the width of the awning. Draw a straight line across the awning inboard of the anticipated grommet locations and a second line inboard of the first by the batten diameter. Hem the ends of the strip, then sew one edge on the outboard line. Fold the strip over, turn the raw edge under $1/2$ inch, and sew this edge on the inboard line to form a pocket. Sew one end closed, insert the batten, and sew the other end closed. Metal electrical conduit (EMT) makes good awning battens, but tape the ends to reduce chafe.

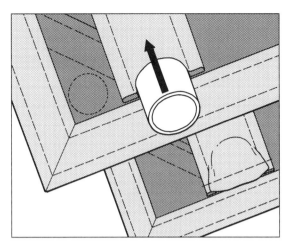

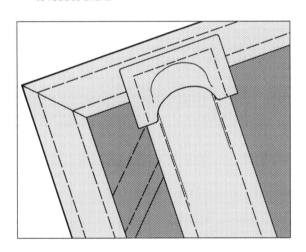

5 You can make battens removable by sewing an overlapping flap over one end of the pocket instead of stitching it closed. Batten pockets also need not fully enclose the batten: 6-inch pockets at either end will hold a batten securely. If the batten telescopes, it can be easily removed from end pockets.

6 Peaked awnings need a ridge rope. Do not install a ridge rope by folding the awning in half and sewing the rope into the fold: this concentrates all the stress on the stitching. The proper way is inside a pocket, and you have a 3-inch-wide strip of canvas set aside just for this purpose. Splice eyes around nylon thimbles in both ends of a length of $3/8$-inch Dacron rope, so that the distance between the eyes is the same as the distance between the planned location of the two center grommets on the awning. Strike a straight line on the underside of the awning between the grommet locations, and capture the ridge rope on this line with the canvas strip and your zipper foot, turning under all raw edges.

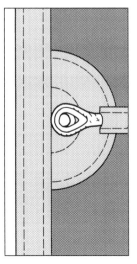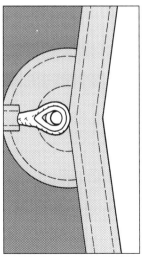

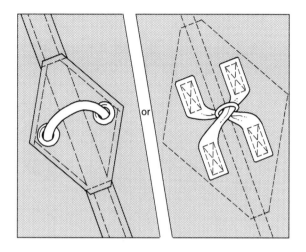

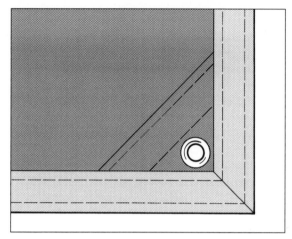

7 Stitch oval or diamond-shaped patches over the ridge rope on the underside of the awning at the lift location(s). If you don't mind two holes in the roof, install grommets in the lift patch on either side of the ridge rope so you can pass a strop through. An alternative is to box-stitch crossed 1-inch straps, with a captured 1-inch brass ring, to the upper side of the awning on either side of the rope. Straps made of tripled canvas will outlive webbing in the sun.

8 Install the perimeter grommets, setting them back far enough from the edge to take full advantage of the reinforcement patches.

EXTERNAL SPREADERS

Minimize wear to your awning by attaching the spreaders to the securing lines rather than to the awning. External spreaders are sometimes attached with eyes and snaphooks, but the easiest method is to put two stopper knots in a tie line and drop it into a slot in the end of the spreader, where tension holds it quite securely. To use this method, you must put solid plugs in the ends of hollow spreaders.

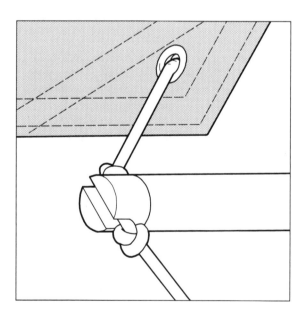

SIDE CURTAINS

Some sailors make side curtains a permanent feature of their harbor awning, rolled up and tied along the edge when not in use. Unfortunately, integral side curtains can double the bulk of an awning. Removable side curtains offer better flexibility. They can be attached with zippers, but lacing allows a single curtain to be located anywhere around the awning's edge.

1 Make lace-on side curtains exactly like a fender skirt, but with grommets spaced every 6 to 8 inches along one side to match the mid position of corresponding grommets in the edge hem of the awning. Corner grommets on the bottom edge allow you to secure the bottom. For additional flexibility install a couple of intermediate grommets on the bottom edge.

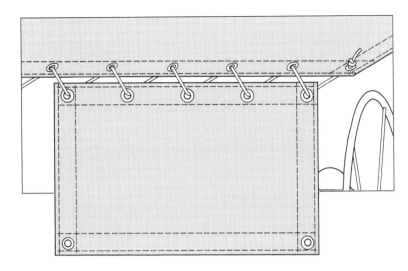

2 Lacing is hardly onerous, but you can easily make the side curtains button to the awning. Cut inch-long pieces of $1/4$-inch hardwood dowel and drill them with two $1/8$-inch holes about $1/2$ inch apart. Thread them as shown with $1/8$-inch braided Dacron flag halyard.

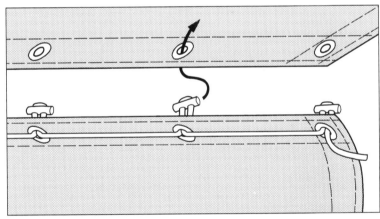

3 To leave side curtains attached when they aren't needed, roll them up and tie them with short lengths of line or webbing (shoe laces are ideal) passing through every third or fourth grommet.

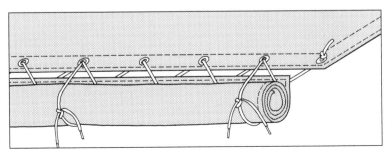

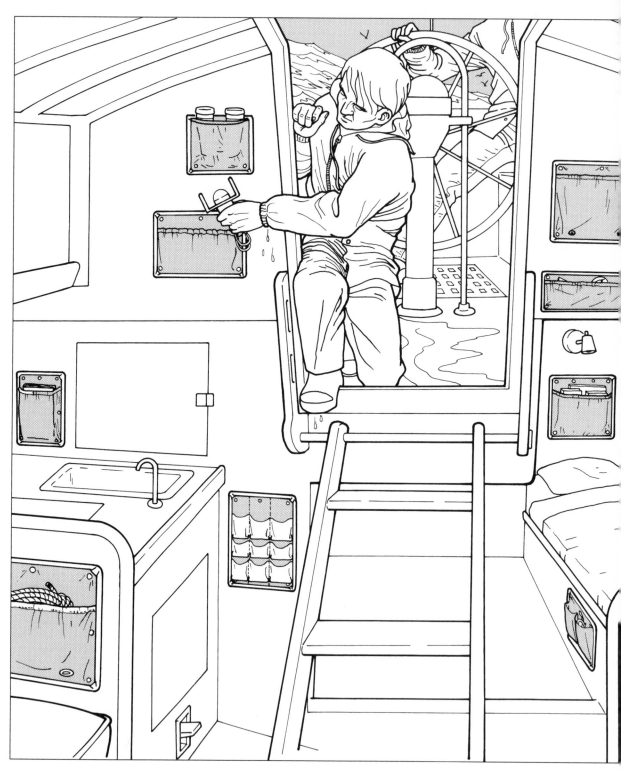

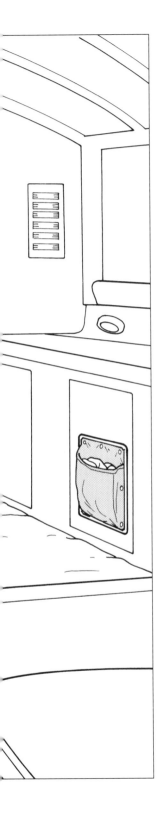

THE POCKET

ockets are just as handy on a boat as they are in jeans, jackets, or kangaroos. Boats have an amazing affinity for gathering small items that then disappear when actually needed. Pockets are marvelous at helping you get a handle on that problem.

Pockets also provide storage possibilities for the odd-shaped spaces and inaccessible nooks on a boat that would otherwise be wasted. Buying a larger boat isn't the only solution to running out of space; with a little ingenuity and a few yards of fabric, you can substantially increase the useful space within the confines of your hull.

Pockets don't just confine: they also protect, holding their contents in a padded embrace. Pockets mounted high in lockers, out of harm's way, can be the safest place for fragile items. On the back of a cabinet door they can quell the rattle of pot lids. Or lying against the hull and stuffed with soft goods, a fabric pocket protects both the hull and the loose items in a locker.

Once you have mastered putting a hem in the perimeter of a flat sheet, the pocket is the next logical step for broadening the value of this new-found skill. In its simplest incarnation, the pocket is nothing more than a doubled flat sheet with the sides sewn together. Make the fold short of the middle and you end up with a flap that can be given grommets for hanging the pocket or snaps for closing it—or both.

In this book we have room to detail only a few of the most useful pocket items, but the variety of ways to take advantage of the pocket's utility aboard a boat is limited only by your imagination. Anytime you are looking for a way to stow an item out of the way or, ironically, to keep it immediately at hand, you will do well to ponder how a pocket might serve as more than a repository for your idle hands.

HANGING STORAGE POCKETS

You can never find the key to the water-fill cap? Sat on another pair of sunglasses? Dive fins come out of the cockpit locker distorted? Easily fabricated hanging canvas pockets can solve all of these problems and dozens more like them.

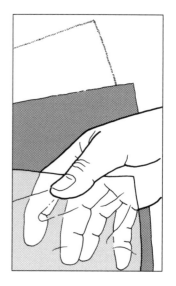

SELECTING THE FABRIC

You need the chafe resistance of treated natural canvas if the pocket will contain heavy items like tools or winch handles. For most other applications, choose acrylic canvas, taking advantage of the color variety to make it easier to remember what is in a specific pocket. For even easier identification, make the pocket from clear vinyl or acrylic canvas with a vinyl front. Ripstop nylon (spinnaker cloth) makes excellent pockets for clothes and other lightweight items. Linens and blankets will stay fresher in open-weave Phifertex bags; Phifertex also makes an excellent laundry bag.

BIND, DON'T HEM

If you hem your canvas before folding it into a pocket, the edges can become excessively bulky. Avoid this by finishing the edges with binding tape. Binding tape is a narrow strip of vinyl or cloth (white Orlon or acrylic in matching colors) with finished edges; ¾-inch is a good general-purpose width. Fold the tape over the raw edge(s) of the canvas and sew it down—with a zigzag stitch if your machine is capable. Dart the tape at corners. Seamed edges in canvas will be stronger if you sew the parts together first, then bind the edges.

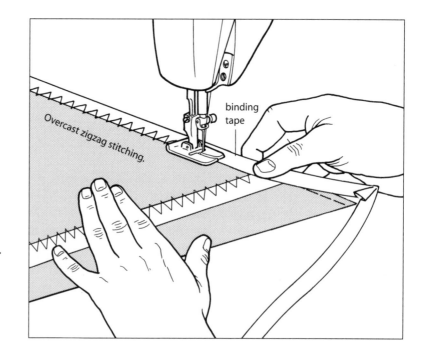

Overcast zigzag stitching.

binding tape

MAKING A POCKET

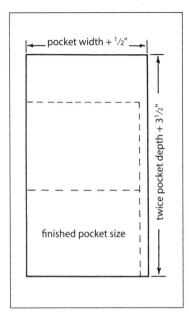

pocket width + ¹/₂"

twice pocket depth + 3¹/₂"

finished pocket size

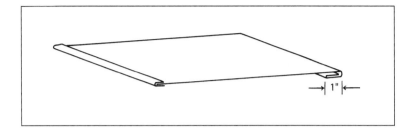

1"

2 Put a 1-inch double-rubbed hem in one end. Hem or bind the opposite end.

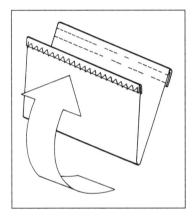

3 With the 1-inch hem to the back, fold the fabric to position the bound edge about 2 inches below the hemmed edge, then seam the sides.

1 Cut a rectangle of fabric ¹/₂ inch wider than the interior width of the planned pocket and about 3¹/₂ inches longer than twice the desired depth.

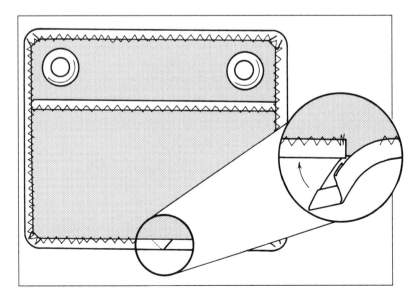

4 Bind the entire perimeter, cutting the end of the binding tape on a diagonal and folding it under to finish. Install #2 spur grommets in the corners of the triple-thickness flap.

CLEAR POCKETS

Make clear vinyl pockets, ideal for manuals and documents and for a conglomeration of small items, as with any other fabric. Binding tape makes the vinyl easier to sew—don't seam vinyl first. Be sure you are using your longest stitch. Mounted clear pockets are more attractive with a canvas back. In this case, cut the front and back separately and assemble them with binding tape. You can leave the top edge of the vinyl raw.

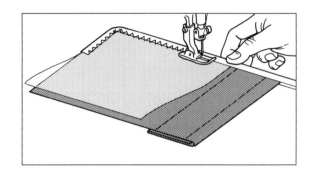

CLOSURES

1 If you want a closing flap rather than one for hanging, omit the double-rubbed hem and reduce the cut size appropriately.

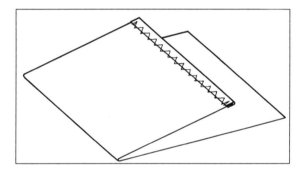

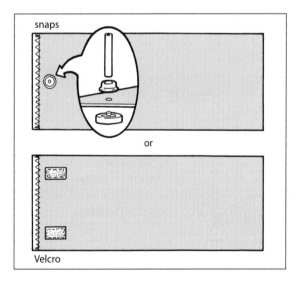

snaps

or

Velcro

2 Install half of your closure in the material before you fold it into a pocket. For snaps, pierce the material with a heated ice pick or awl, fit the stud, and set it with a snap setter. For a Velcro closure, sew around the perimeter of a horizontal strip of loop tape. If the flap needs to be adjustable, substitute two vertical strips.

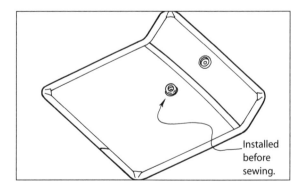

Installed before sewing.

3 Finish the pocket, fill it to see where the flap half of the closure belongs, then install the closure in the flap.

ZIPPER POCKETS

Pockets made from canvas or clear vinyl that close with a zipper—like a bank bag—are especially useful aboard a boat. A YKK #5 plastic zipper is recommended, but you can also use a common dress zipper.

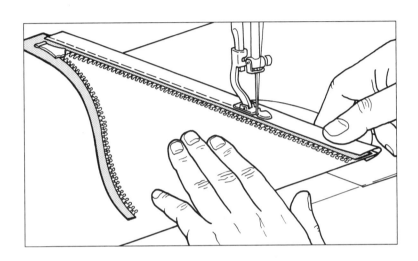

1 When you cut the material, omit the flap altogether. Use your zipper foot and a zipper slightly shorter than the pocket's width. Unzip the zipper and, with the zipper pull tab down, align the cloth edge of each half with an end edge of the fabric and sew them together with binding tape.

2 Bind the open sides, turning the binding tape under at both ends.

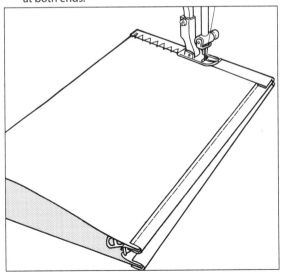

3 Turn the finished bag inside out.

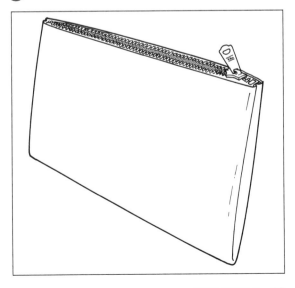

TOOL ROLLS

Square toolboxes are often a poor fit in round sailboats. By contrast, canvas tool rolls are easy to stow, keep tools quiet, provide instant accounting, and can be oiled to provide rust protection. The only fabric choice for tool rolls is treated canvas.

1 With a cloth tape, measure the surface-to-surface distance over the widest point of each tool you want to include in the roll. Add $^1/_2$ inch to each measurement and record them. Add all these dimensions together plus 2 inches to determine the cut width. The cut length should be 3 inches more than twice the length of the longest tool in the roll.

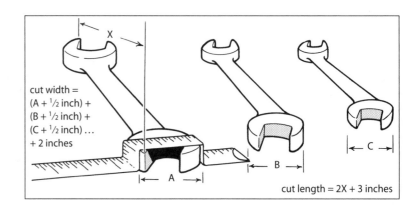

2 Arrange the tools on the fabric from longest to shortest and fold the fabric to pocket them. Push each tool down to seat it against the fold, then fold the top of the front diagonally to expose enough of each tool to allow it to be easily identified and removed. Cut the fabric on this second fold line.

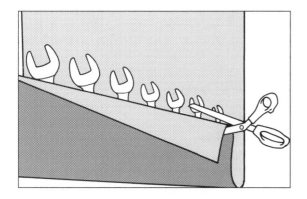

3 Fold the flap diagonally over the tops of the tools and cut away excess canvas to make the width of the flap even. Align the edge of the flap on one side by trimming it, and on the other side by trimming 1½ inches from the side of the pocket.

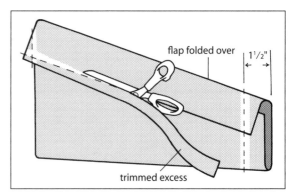

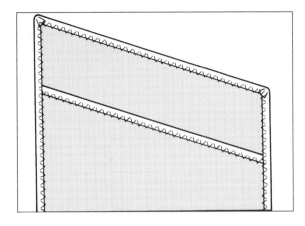

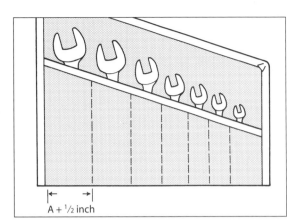

4 Trace the angled edge of the pocket onto the back panel to mark it, then remove the tools and bind this edge. Fold the pocket to the trace lines and seam the sides, then bind over the raw edges.

5 Along the front face, mark the width of each pocket per your recorded measurements, then extend a perpendicular line to the top of the pocket. Run a line of straight stitches on each pencil line, and be sure to backstitch the upper ends.

6 On the long side of the roll, just above half the *pocket* height, sew the middle of a shoelace or a length of cloth binding tape to the edge with three rows of stitching. This is the tie, and you can determine the appropriate length for it by putting the tools in the roll and rolling it up. If you use binding tape, hem the ends.

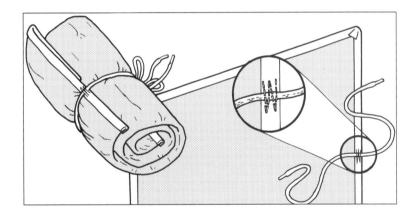

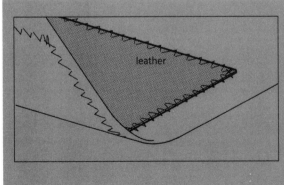

leather

LEATHER LINING

YOU CAN GREATLY EXTEND the life of a pocket that holds heavy items, such as a tool roll, by lining the bottom of the pocket with leather. Before folding and stitching the pocket, center a 3-inch-wide strip of leather on the fold line and sew it down all around with an overcasting zigzag stitch; then finish the pocket normally. This can also be done along the flap's fold line for the same purpose.

SHEET BAGS

With the sails cranked in, there can easily be 100 feet or more of sheet tail jumbled in the cockpit. Aside from aesthetics, a pile of line can be a safety hazard. Get control of this situation with a sheet bag or two. You can use a standard hanging pocket as a sheet bag, but a slightly different construction technique yields a pocket better suited for the bulk.

1 In this bag, the front and back are separate pieces. Cut the back to your desired finished dimension, plus $1\frac{1}{2}$ extra inches in the height dimension. The back piece of an 18 by 10 bag—a good size—would be 18 by $11\frac{1}{2}$ inches. Cut the front piece the same height but 4 inches wider (22 by $11\frac{1}{2}$ inches).

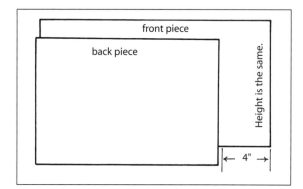

2 Put a $\frac{3}{4}$-inch (both folds) double-rubbed hem in the top of the back piece. Put a 2-inch *casing* in the top edge of the front, with $\frac{1}{4}$ inch of the raw edge turned under. A casing differs from a double-rubbed hem only in the absence of the second row of stitching near the fold.

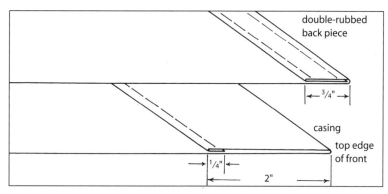

3 Mark a length of $\frac{1}{4}$-inch bungee cord the designed width of your bag. Feed it through the casing and sew the end about $\frac{1}{2}$ inch from the edge. (If you can't get bungee under the foot of your machine, use 2-inch waistband elastic doubled lengthwise.) Pull the other end until the mark is outside, then sew this end down the same way. Trim the bungee at the stitching at both ends.

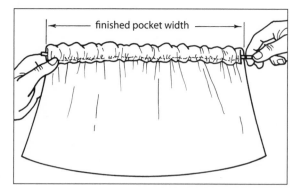

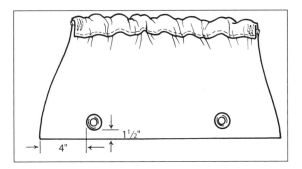

4 Install grommets in the front, placing their edges $1\frac{1}{2}$ inches from the bottom and 4 inches from the sides. These are drains, but you don't want them to interfere with the bottom seam.

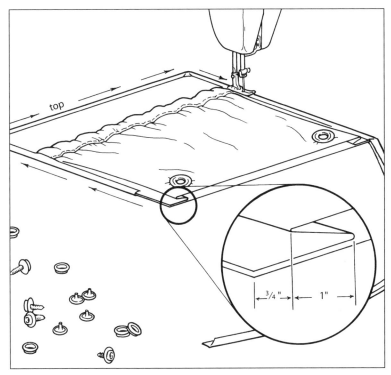

5 Bind the two halves together. Begin on one side and sew toward and across the top. When you get to the bottom corner, take out half of the excess front material with a 1-inch *pleat* positioned $3/4$ inch from the side. Bind across the bottom, putting a matching pleat on the opposite side.

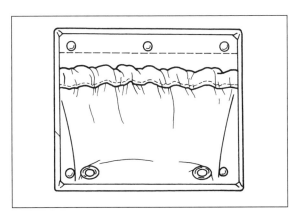

6 Install snap fasteners in all corners and one in the middle of the top flap. Screw matching studs to the boat where you want to mount the bag. If you put a couple of additional studs inside the cockpit locker, you will also have a perfect place to stow sheets when they aren't in use.

MULTI-POCKET BAGS

Drawer cabinets, those gizmos with a dozen or so little clear-plastic drawers for nuts and bolts and little parts, useful though they might be, aren't very practical aboard a sailboat. The multi-pocket bag is an effective alternative. Use acrylic or treated canvas for the back, clear vinyl (from a roll) for the front.

1 Determine where the bag will be mounted—on the inside of a cabinet door, for example—and cut the canvas back with a 1-inch allowance on the height dimension.

2 Determine the number of pockets you want, reserving ½ inch of the canvas at the top and bottom for mounting. Be sure the pockets will be wide enough or shallow enough to allow you to reach the bottom. Cut strips of vinyl—one strip for each row of pockets. Determine the strip lengths by adding to the canvas width 4 inches for every pocket across. In other words, if you plan three pockets across a 15-inch piece of canvas, cut the vinyl strips 27 inches long $[15 + (3 \times 4) = 27]$.

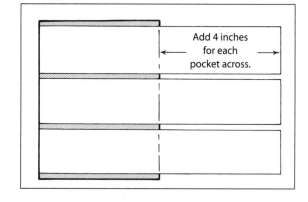

Add 4 inches for each pocket across.

3 To provide sturdy mounting strips, align lengths of Dacron or nylon webbing with the top and bottom edges of the canvas and sew them near the inner edge of the webbing. Half-inch webbing is ideal, but wider is fine if that's what you have.

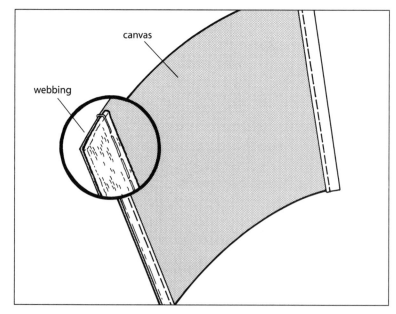

canvas

webbing

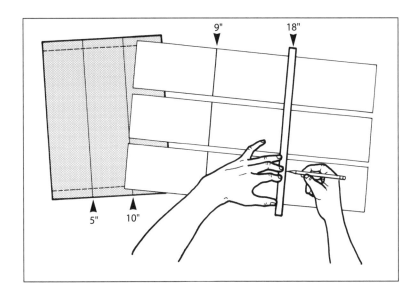

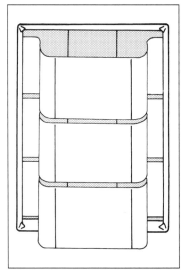

4 Assuming equal pockets, divide the canvas with vertical pencil lines (on the opposite side of the fabric from the webbing) into the number of pockets across—here with lines at 5 and 10 inches. Similarly mark the plastic strips into the same number of equal divisions; in this case the divisions are 9 inches apart (27 ÷ 3 = 9).

5 Abut the vinyl strips long edge to long edge, and align them with one edge of the canvas and ½ inch from the top and bottom. Bind them to the canvas, then continue with the binding all the way around, capturing the free edges of the webbing at the top and bottom, and the opposite ends of the vinyl strips on the other side.

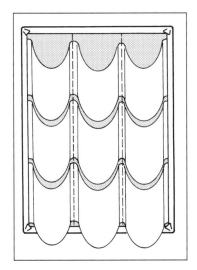

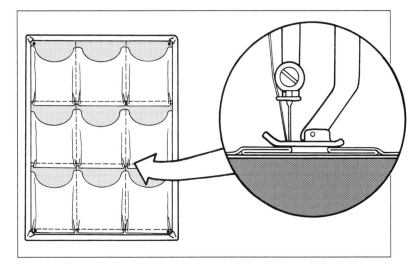

6 Align the divider marks on the vinyl with those on the canvas and sew them together on the lines.

7 Pleat the pockets at the bottom and sew across. Melt holes on the four corners and mount the bag with screws and finishing washers.

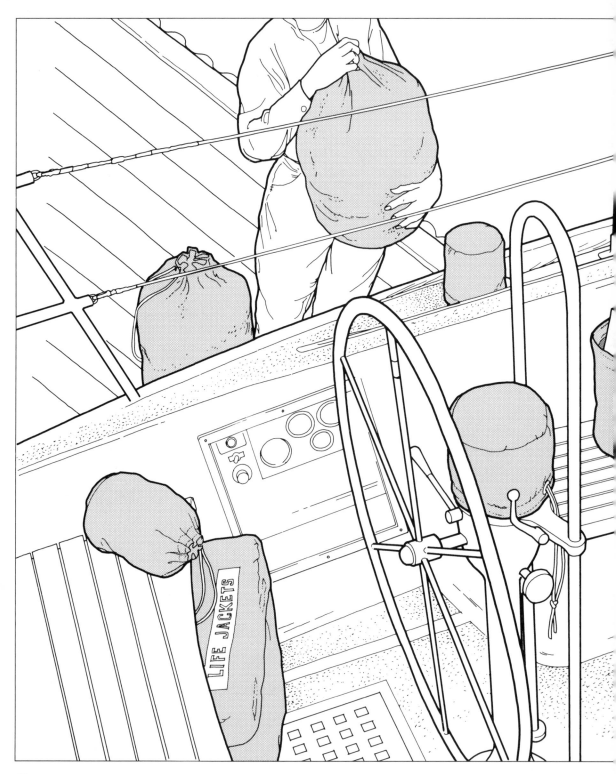

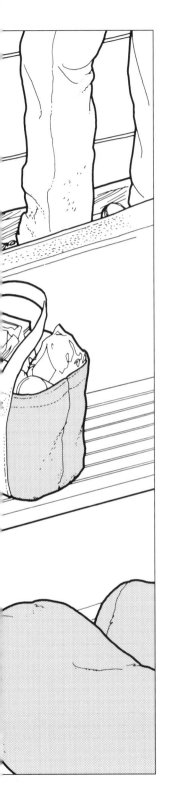

THE BAG

Not everything you want to stow, carry, or protect will fit into a pocket. Bulky items need a bag with a two-dimensional bottom. The distinction here is easier to understand if you think of the pocket as a canvas envelope and the bag as a canvas box.

The box-like shape of a canvas bag makes it extremely handy for transporting items to and from the boat. Grocery bags also serve, but who hasn't had the experience of the wet bottom of a paper bag suddenly turning loose? If it happens as you are passing the bag aboard, it can be a major event.

Canvas tote bags are readily available at reasonable prices, some intended specifically for marine use. The drawback to ready-made bags is that they are too often not the best size for the use you have in mind. A typical chandlery tote is 6 or 7 inches wide, making a spool of rope or a pressure cooker an odd fit. And while a pillowcase may be fine for transporting soiled linens and towels, getting the laundered and folded items back aboard neatly calls for a bag big enough to swallow the stack. Such a bag is hard to purchase but easy to construct.

Turn a bag bottom-up and you have a hood. Whether it is a hatch, a binnacle, or an outboard motor you want to protect, the cover is simply a bag of the appropriate dimension with a drawstring, snaps, or other fastening system around the opening.

Making a canvas bag is only slightly more involved than making a pocket, as you will see soon enough. By making one or two of the items detailed in this chapter, you will add to your comprehension and skill level. At the very least make a couple of tote bags for your boat; you will find them so handy that additional bags will soon be on your list of things to do.

ONE-PIECE TOTE BAG

Every sailor can find a good use for a canvas tote bag. A bag measuring 1 foot on every side is extraordinarily versatile, but a larger bag may be better for clothes or linens. Conversely, the weight of a cubic foot of hand tools may dictate a smaller bag for a tool tote. Treated canvas, because of its chafe-resistance and strength, is the best fabric for tote bags.

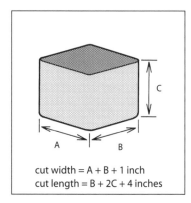

cut width = A + B + 1 inch
cut length = B + 2C + 4 inches

1 Determine the bottom and height dimensions of the finished bag. Cut the fabric 1 inch wider than half the bottom circumference, and 4 inches longer than the narrower bottom dimension plus twice the height of the bag. For a cubic-foot bag, that is 25 inches by 40 inches.

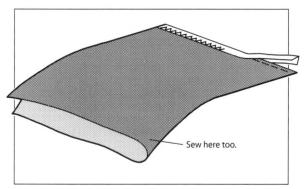

Sew here too.

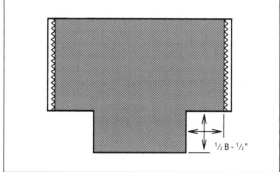

$\frac{1}{2}$ B - $\frac{1}{2}$"

2 Fold the fabric in half across the long dimension and run seams ½ inch from the side edges to form a pocket. Bind the seamed edges.

3 Cut square notches at the corners at the folded edge, making their equal sides ½ inch less than half the narrower bottom dimension. Measure the notch from the fold and from the seams, *not* the edge of the cloth.

PATCH POCKETS

A POCKET OR TWO ON THE INSIDE OR OUTSIDE of your tote bags will keep small items from getting lost at the bottom. Cut a piece of canvas an inch or so larger than the desired pocket. Rub a ½-inch fold on all the edges, then double-rub the top edge (catching the two side folds) and sew in this hem. Now place the pocket wherever you want it on the bag—with the folded edges inside—and sew around three sides. A vertical row of stitches in the middle of a large, loose pocket will give you two smaller but tighter pockets.

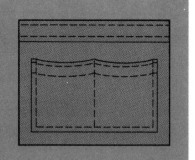

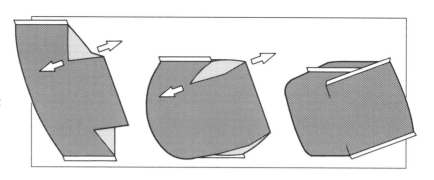

4 Separate the inside corners of the notches, pulling them apart until the notches become straight slits. Seam the slits $1\frac{1}{2}$ inch from the raw edges, and bind them.

5 Turn the finished bag rightside out and put a $1\frac{1}{2}$-inch double-rubbed hem around the top edge.

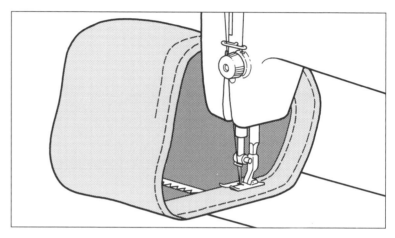

6 Sew $1\frac{1}{2}$-inch webbing to the sides for handles. For strength and durability make the handles pass across (under) the bottom. Mark two parallel lines from hem to hem about a quarter of the bag's width from each side. In a single continuous length, align the webbing to the lines and sew it to the bag along both edges. For carrying ease the handles should loop at least a foot above the bag.

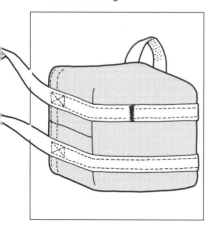

RIGID BOTTOM

SAILORS OFTEN PREFER the rigidity of a box for transporting paint and other liquids, but a bag with a rigid bottom can be just as secure and a lot easier to tote. Make a canvas pocket the size of the bottom of the bag, with a $\frac{1}{2}$-inch flap along the long dimension. Cut a piece of hardboard (Masonite) to fit tightly inside the pocket. Place the empty pocket—flap side up—flat in the bottom of the bag and sew it in place along the flap. Turn the bag inside out and insert the hardboard, then reverse the bag again and fold the rigid bottom down into place. If you want rigid sides as well, find a box that will just fit inside the bag.

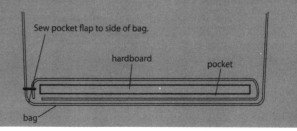

Sew pocket flap to side of bag.

hardboard

pocket

bag

HATCH COVER

If you want to cover a modern flush hatch, you need a hemmed flat sheet with snap fasteners in the four corners, but for a traditional hatch that stands proud, you need a hood—essentially a shallow bag. Acrylic canvas is the fabric of choice: It is UV-resistant and will match the boat's other canvas covers. Attach the hood with snaps, or with a drawstring if you prefer not to screw studs to your hatch.

SNAP-ON COVER

1 Measure from one bottom edge, over the hatch and back to the other bottom edge. Do this in both directions and add 3-inch hem allowances to get the cut size.

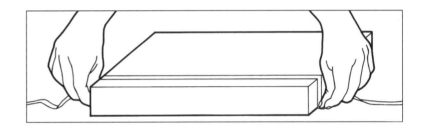

2 Drape the canvas over the hatch and crease it with your thumb to mark the corners.

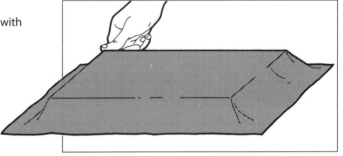

3 Fold the canvas diagonally at one corner to align adjoining edges; the corner mark should fall on the fold. About ¼ inch beyond the mark, run a row of stitches perpendicular to the raw edges. Repeat for the remaining three corners. These are called *darts*.

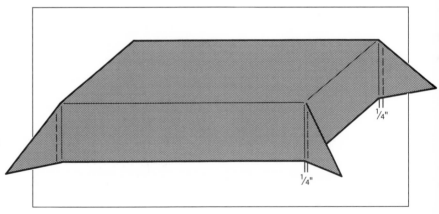

¼"

¼"

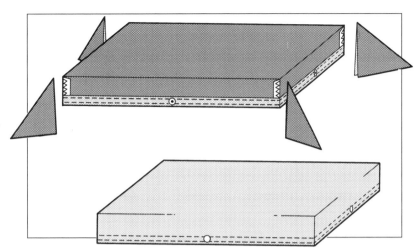

4 Check for fit and move the seams in or out if necessary. When the cover is snug (but not too tight), cut off the excess fabric beyond the seams and bind the edges. Put a ¾-inch (both folds) double-rubbed hem (inside) all around and install snap fasteners.

DRAWSTRING COVER

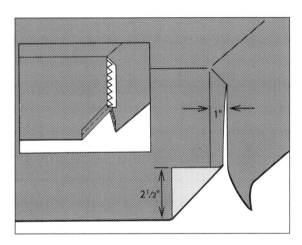

1 Increase the hem allowance to 4 inches. *Before* sewing the corner seams, cut excess material off 1 inch beyond the corner marks. Turn the bottom corners back 2½ inches and sew them down. Trim the cloth parallel to the stitching. Now seam and bind the corners.

2 Fold the edges ½ inch, then 1 inch, and stitch along the inside fold only to put a 1-inch casing in the sides for the drawstring. Tape a length of ⅛-inch flag halyard to a piece of stiff wire and thread the line through the casing until both ends exit at the same corner.

3 Turn the cover rightside out and fit it over the hatch. Pull the ends of the drawstring to fold the cover under the bottom edge, then tie the ends together. If you don't want to tie the cover each time, use bungee rather than flag halyard, but your cover won't be quite as secure.

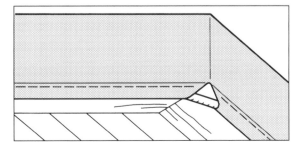

TWO-PIECE DUFFEL BAG

DRAWING A CIRCLE

THE DIAMETER OF MOST duffels will be beyond the capacity of a drawing compass. Tie two loops in a length of thread so that the distance between the loops is equal to the *radius* (half the diameter) of the circle you want to draw. Slip a straight pin through one loop and stick the pin into the cloth where you want the center of the circle. Holding the pin upright with one hand, insert the lead of a pencil into the other loop, then trace your circle by keeping the thread taut as you mark.

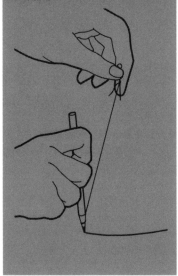

Duffel bags differ from tote bags in that their primary function is to contain rather than carry. They come in all sizes, from a small ditty bag for the ship's clothespins to a large sailbag for the drifter, but their construction is essentially the same. They are traditionally cylindrical because a circular bottom is the best at evenly distributing the load, but you can just as easily make the bottom another shape. They also traditionally close with a drawstring, but for use as luggage it is now more common to enclose the open end and put a zipper in the side. For a drawstring bag, select a fabric that will gather readily, such as oxford nylon.

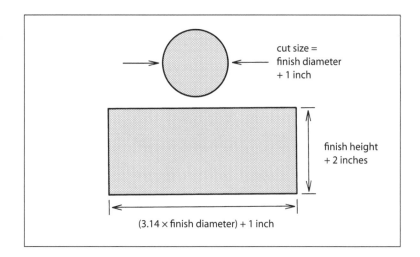

cut size = finish diameter + 1 inch

finish height + 2 inches

(3.14 × finish diameter) + 1 inch

1 Cut the circular bottom piece 1 inch larger than the finish diameter of the bag. The dimensions for the rectangular piece are 1 inch more than 3.14 (π) times the finish diameter and 2 inches more than the finish height. A ditty bag 8 inches in diameter and 10 inches deep requires a 9-inch circle of fabric and a rectangle 12 inches by 26⅛ inches.

2 Fold the rectangle in half and seam and bind the edges opposite the fold to form a tube.

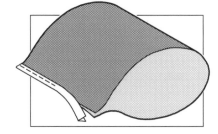

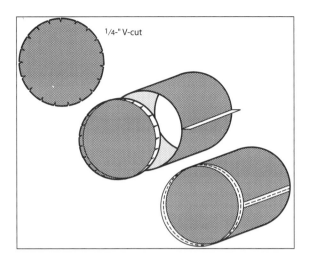

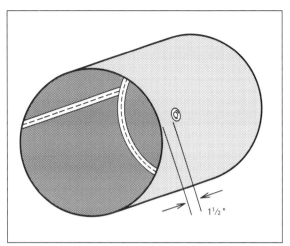

3 Put a series of ¼-inch V-cuts around the perimeter of the circular piece. Fit the circle into one end of the tube and pin or staple it in position; seam tape or glue probably won't hold. Sew the pieces together ½ inch from the edge. Remove the pins or staples and bind the seam.

4 Turn the bag rightside out and install a grommet for the drawstring to exit, placing the outside *edge* of the grommet 1½ inches from the raw edge of the bag's mouth. For a large bag, install a second grommet on the opposite side of the bag; large bags close easier with two drawstrings.

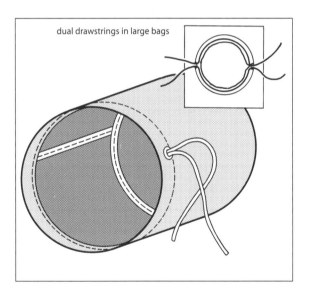

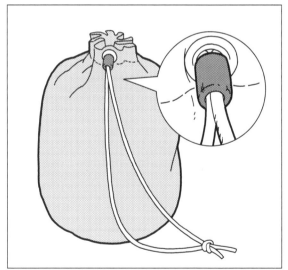

5 Thread the drawstring(s) through the grommet(s) so that the ends are outside and a bight of line is inside. Fold the edge to form a 1-inch casing with the drawstring inside and sew it closed, taking care not to let the needle catch the string.

6 A tight-fitting wooden bead slipped over the ends of the drawstring will hold the bag closed, or use a figure-8 knot. Tie the bitter ends of the drawstring(s) together.

WINCH COVER

No one claims that covered winches last longer, but they do require less maintenance. The time required to make the covers described here should be less than the time to tear down, clean, and lubricate a pair of winches one time. And these particular covers have the advantage of going on as easy as a baseball cap.

1 Using acrylic canvas, make a duffel bag (see previous project) just large enough to slip over and fully cover the winch. Omit the grommet and the drawstring, and add a second row of stitches near the fold of the casing to make it a double-rubbed hem. Omit the binding on the bottom seam.

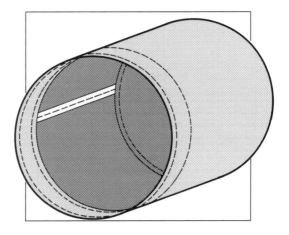

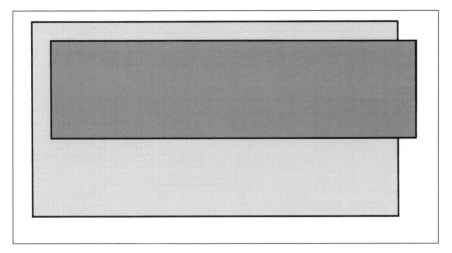

2 Cut a second rectangle of cloth the same length as the first but half the width. This piece should be softer cloth than acrylic canvas—oxford nylon is ideal.

3 Put a 1-inch casing in one long edge of the narrow rectangle. Feed ¼-inch bungee (or doubled waistband elastic) through the casing.

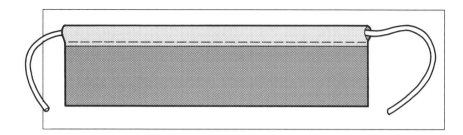

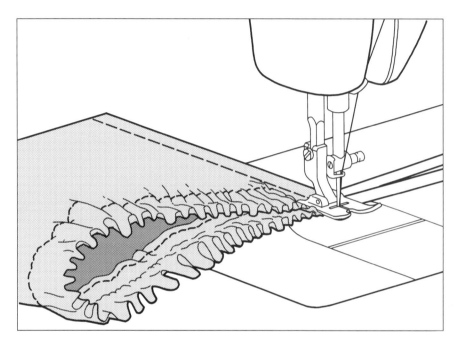

4 Fold the cloth in half and seam the ends together, stopping the machine—*with the needle down*—just before the foot reaches the elastic. Pull the ends of the elastic like a drawstring until the diameter of the tube is about halved, then continue the seam, sewing back and forth over the elastic several times to secure the ends. Snip off the excess elastic and bind the seam.

5 Slip the inside-out bag through the tube and align the raw edges. Seam and bind the tube to the bag. When you turn the bag rightside out, it now has an internal elastic skirt. Reach inside the cover and spread the elastic over the winch to hold the cover in place.

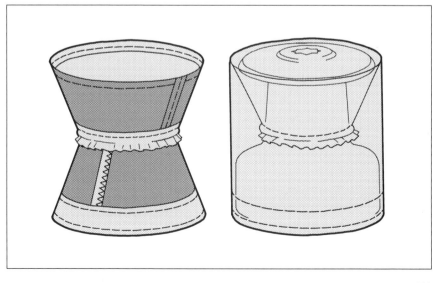

LIFE-JACKET BOX

In 1995 the law changed to require wearable flotation devices aboard virtually all boats. Flotation cushions are no longer adequate even for the dinghy. That may mean you are carrying additional life jackets aboard your boat. In any case, it is a sign of good seamanship to have life jackets not just aboard but readily accessible.

A soft box secured in the cockpit or on deck can keep jackets from becoming buried in a locker and assure they will be instantly at hand in an emergency. You can make a jacket-storage bag from acrylic canvas, but the material of choice is Weblon—a nylon-reinforced vinyl.

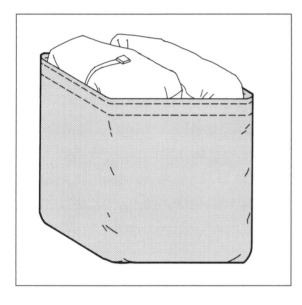

1 Stack all your life jackets as compactly as possible and determine the size bag required to contain them. They should fill the bag to the top. Fabricate a one-piece tote bag (see page 64) to these dimensions. Omit the handles, but add straps or fasteners as needed to secure the bag in the selected location.

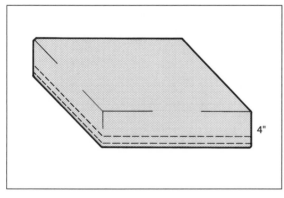

4"

2 Using the bottom dimensions of the tote bag, fabricate a hatch cover (see page 66) with 4-inch sides. This is the lid of your box.

3 Sew several strips of 1-inch Velcro hook tape along the inside edge of the lid at both ends and on one side. Slip the lid over the bag to mark the locations for the corresponding strips of loop tape, then sew them to the bag.

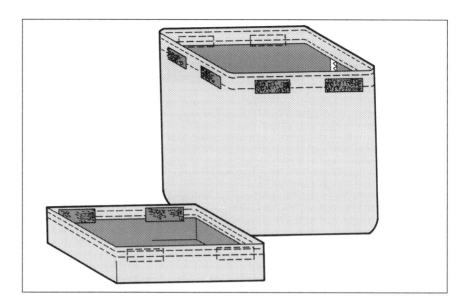

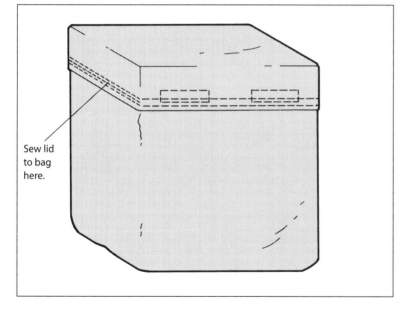

Sew lid to bag here.

4 Carefully fit the side of the bag without Velcro onto the corresponding side of the lid and sew them together with a row of stitches near the bottom edge of the lid. Fill the box with life jackets and close the lid.

THE CLOSED BOX

The life-jacket "box" ending "The Bag" is actually two bags, not a closed box. The distinction is easy to make: a rectangular bag has five sides, a closed box has six.

It would seem that all we have to do to make a bag into a closed box is add a side, but do *just* that and you better make sure that whatever you want the box to contain is already in there. Also the seams, or at least the last one, are going to be on the outside because there is no way to turn a closed box inside out.

The solution to this is to put an opening in one of the sides. The opening allows you to reverse the box so all seams are on the inside, and it allows you to fill the box *after* you sew it. Some kind of closure will be needed. This is most often a zipper, but you can also close the opening with snaps, Velcro, or even lacing.

Loose cushions are nothing more than a closed box stuffed with padding. This is true whether they are settee cushions, bunk cushions, or cockpit cushions, whether they are an inch or 6 inches thick, and whether they are perfectly square or have the arrowhead shape of the V-bunk. The construction of a cover for an odd-shaped cushion is exactly the same as for one with all right angles.

If you made a duffel bag from "The Bag," you already have *almost* all the skills needed to re-cover old cushions or make new ones (see page 68). You may still need some help getting the top to align squarely with the bottom; installing a zipper will be easier if you know a couple of tricks; and you should know how to make and install piping to give the seams a finished look. But none of these added requirements are any more difficult than those we have already mastered. All are fully explained in this chapter.

The closed box is the neatest of the canvas containers and surely the most satisfying to construct. Master it and you can take on any onboard canvas project with confidence.

Blankets, sweaters, and other bulky items can quickly fill limited stowage space. At the same time, most settees—designed to fit the space, not your back—are too upright for comfort. Help both problems by storing blankets and sweaters in a canvas bolster that doubles as lumbar support. Choose a fabric that feels comfortable, preferably one you can throw in the wash.

1 Make a size determination based on planned use or by measuring the bundle you want to enclose. A fat bolster at the end of a settee provides a comfortable arm rest. For lumbar support, limit the diameter to about 6 inches. Cut two identical circles with a 1-inch seam allowance. Also allow 1 inch on the "length" dimension of the rectangular piece and add the total *width* of the zipper to the "around" dimension. A bolster 8 inches in diameter and 16 inches long would require two 9-inch circles of fabric and a rectangle measuring 17 by 26⅝, assuming a 1½-inch-wide zipper (see step 1 of "Two-Piece Duffel Bag," page 68).

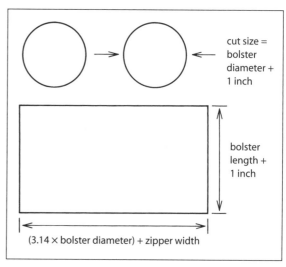

cut size = bolster diameter + 1 inch

bolster length + 1 inch

(3.14 × bolster diameter) + zipper width

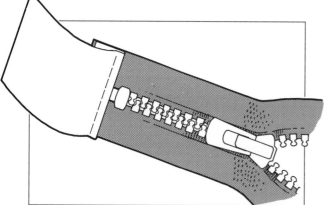

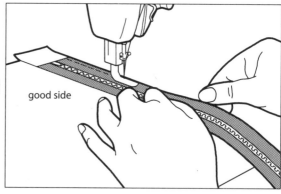

good side

2 Select a zipper slightly shorter than the finished length of the bolster. The tape that extends beyond the teeth at either end of the zipper should provide an overall length longer than the bolster's finished length. If it doesn't, extend the closed end with webbing or a strip of fabric.

3 For perfect zipper alignment, place the zipper—tab down—on top of the good side of the fabric and align the two edge-to-edge and centered side-to-side. Sew them together near the edge.

4 Fold the material so the fold lies down the center of the zipper. Use the zipper foot to topstitch the fabric parallel to the fold, catching both layers of fabric and the zipper tape, but taking care not to sew close enough to the zipper's teeth to interfere with the operation of the slider.

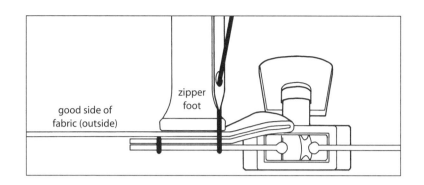

good side of fabric (outside)

zipper foot

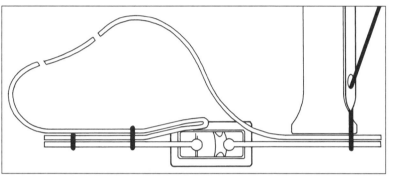

5 Fold the fabric in half inside out, aligning the exposed edge of the zipper with the raw edge of the cloth, and sew them together. Unzip the zipper, then fold and topstitch this side just like the other one.

6 Zip the two halves back together with the tube inside out. Notch the two circles and sew them in the ends exactly like sewing the bottom in a duffel (see "The Bag"). Open the zipper and turn the finished bolster rightside out.

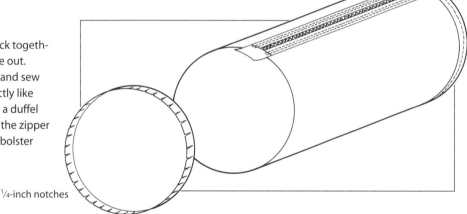

¹/₄-inch notches

ZIPPERS

FOR OUTSIDE USE SELECT only YKK #10 Delrin zippers. Below deck the smaller YKK #5 zipper may be preferable. Complete zippers—called jacket zippers—allow the separation of both halves and come in a range of lengths. Zipper is also available in continuous length—called zipper tape—for applications that don't require separation, such as a bolster, bag, or cushion closure. You can use a jacket zipper for these applications, but zipper tape may be cheaper. Use only plastic sliders aboard a boat.

ZIPPERED DUFFEL BAG

The only difference between a bolster and a zippered duffel is the handle and the choice of fabric. Make duffel bags from acrylic canvas.

1 Strike a pair of lines around the finished bag 3 or 4 inches either side of the center. Sew a continuous length of webbing to the bag on these two lines so the handle loops overlap at the zipper by 5 or 6 inches. Stitch the handles only to the lower half of the bag.

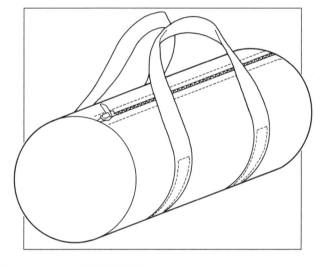

2 If you want padded handles, use 2-inch webbing. Mark the center of the handle loops. Cut two 6-inch lengths of $3/8$-inch rubber hose and use your zipper foot to sew them into a fold in the webbing and centered on the mark. Sew across the webbing at the ends of the hose.

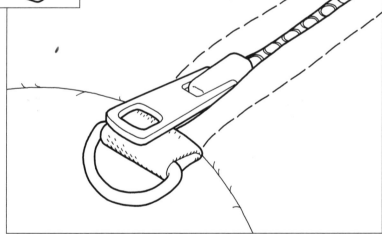

3 To make your duffel lockable, fold a short length of webbing around a small D-ring and sew it into the end seam at the "open" end of the zipper *at the time you are installing that end*. A small lock between the slider tab and the D-ring will prevent casual opening of the bag.

PIPING

You may find a bolster more attractive finished with piping, also called *welt cord*. *Piping* is a fabric bead that gives exposed seams a finished look and effectively hides the stitching even when the seam is under stress. Extruded piping is available in a variety of colors and sizes for use with vinyl fabrics. For woven cloth, you are more likely to make your own piping by wrapping a strip of matching or contrasting cloth around cord.

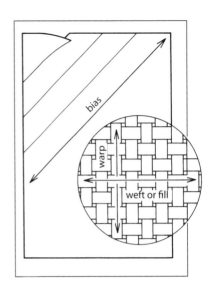

1 Piping generally handles better if the fabric is cut on the bias, i.e., diagonally (see page 29, "Measuring and Cutting"), but to save fabric the strips are often cut from scrap, which usually means with the grain. It isn't likely to matter much, and if you have a patterned fabric, you may want to cut it with the grain anyway to match the pattern.

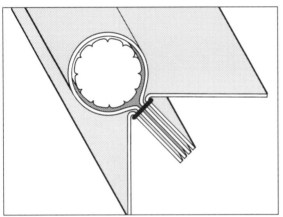

2 Piping size can vary from subtle to bold, and you can buy appropriate cord from a fabric supplier. Keep in mind that the piping will be larger than the cord alone. The width of the fabric strips depends upon the size of the cord and your preferred seam allowance. Experiment with a scrap before you cut all the strips. Ideally you want the edges of the piping to align with the edges of the fabric when you sew the seams. For an attractive and easy-to-make contrasting piping, simply fold binding tape around flag halyard.

3 Cut all the strips for the needed piping and sew them end to end. A diagonal seam is preferred. For the joined pieces to align properly, position them perpendicular with their pointed corners extending beyond the strip edges by approximately the seam width. Butterfly the seam.

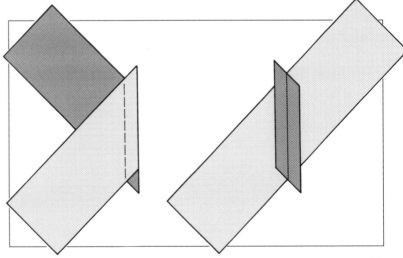

4 You can pin, staple, or glue the fabric around the cord to baste it, but the surest and often quickest method is to sew it. Place the row of stitches well away from the cord so they won't show in the finished seam.

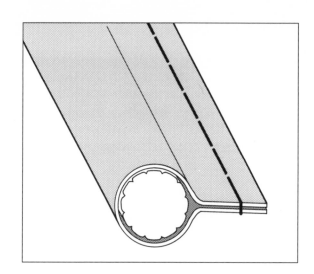

5 Install piping or welt by simply sewing it between the two pieces of fabric being seamed. If you cut the strips to the right width, all the raw edges will align. Use a zipper foot to place the stitches as close to the cord as possible. This makes the piping neatly tight and hides any basting stitches. Slash the raw edges to let the cord turn corners easily.

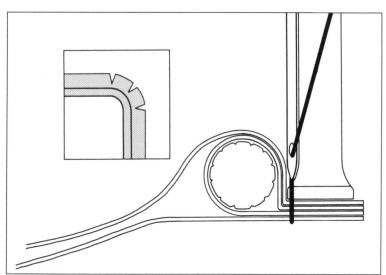

COCKPIT CUSHIONS

ockpit cushions provide a good opportunity for a first foray into upholstery. Good cockpit cushions—meaning made of closed-cell foam and covered with weather-resistant fabric—are a marvelous addition to any boat.

The best fabric for cockpit cushions is acrylic canvas. Besides being weather-resistant, it resists staining, is comfortable against the skin, and dries quickly. Avoid dark colors if the cushions will have strong sun exposure.

Another popular fabric for cockpit cushions is Phifertex. This open-weave fabric comes in a wide variety of light colors designed for outdoor use. It doesn't shield the foam from moisture, but since closed-cell foam doesn't absorb water—an essential characteristic for outdoor cushions—this foam and

fabric combination dries very quickly. The vinyl coating does tend to yellow with age.

Reinforced vinyl is another choice; it wears well, cleans easily, and is waterproof. But vinyl tends to be sticky and uncomfortable against bare skin. Even open-weave Phifertex can exhibit this trait. Solid reinforced vinyls also tend to trap moisture against the foam, culturing mold and mildew inside the cover. Some vinyls quickly harden and crack in the sun.

Use only closed-cell foam for cockpit cushions. Typically made of ethylene vinyl acetate (EVA), closed-cell foam is readily available in 1- and 2-inch thicknesses (approximately). The thicker size will be more comfortable.

1 Cut paper patterns for the best cushion configuration for your cockpit. Multiple cushions can be better than trying to pad the entire area with two cushions. Smaller cushions are easier to stow and can do double duty as back cushions. Cushions slightly larger than the hatch underneath allow locker access without disturbing the other seating. Do try to avoid separations in the most likely seating locations. Note the back edge on each pattern to help later in zipper placement.

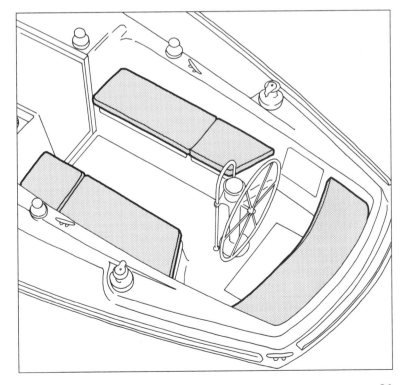

2 Closed-cell foam shrinks with age, so cut each cushion ½ inch larger all around than your paper patterns. Mark the foam and cut on the lines with a just-sharpened fillet knife, drawing the knife in the same direction several times for each cut.

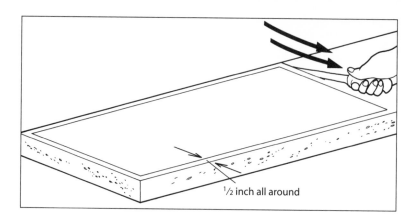

½ inch all around

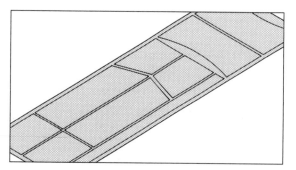

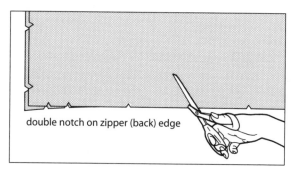

double notch on zipper (back) edge

3 Each cushion requires a matching top and bottom, but if your material has a "good" side, be sure the top and bottom are mirror images, not duplicates. Use the paper patterns to lay out the material, again adding ½ inch all around, but this time as a seam allowance. It is a good idea to lay out all the pieces—including the strips for the sides and the piping—before you make any cuts.

4 With the two cut pieces aligned good side to good side, make matching shallow notches in their hem allowances a couple of inches from either side of the corners. Put similar notches every foot or so along the sides. These notches will help you align the top and bottom when you sew the cover together. Double-notch one corner on the zipper edge for easy orientation.

5 The strip of cloth that joins the top and bottom is called the *boxing*. It is easier to fabricate the boxing in two sections, one containing the zipper. Cut two strips of fabric a couple of inches longer than the length of the zipper and 1⅛ inches wider than half the thickness of the foam (assuming your zipper is 1½ inches wide). The zipper should be slightly shorter than the back side of the cushion. Sew the zipper, edge aligned and tab down, to the good side of one of the strips, then fold the strip along the center of the zipper and sew it again. Attach the second strip to the opposite edge of the zipper in the same manner.

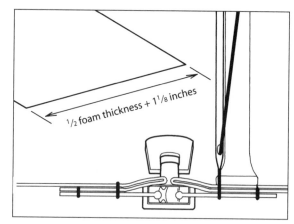

½ foam thickness + 1⅛ inches

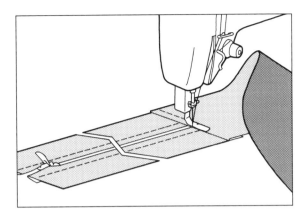

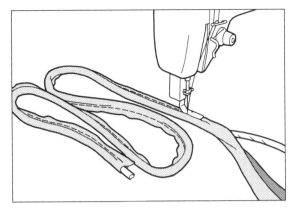

6 Subtract the length of the zipper assembly from the circumference of the cushion, then add about 3 inches to get the length of the remaining boxing. Cut this strip ¾ inch wider than the foam thickness. With a ½-inch seam allowance on each side, this provides a finished width ¼ less than the foam, which improves the cover's fit. Hem one end of the boxing and sew it to the zipper assembly, taking care to keep the edges straight.

7 Cut the needed strips of fabric for the piping, sew them together, and baste them shut with the cord inside. Make up enough piping for all the cushions in a continuous length, cutting it as you use it. Extruded vinyl piping eliminates this step for vinyl or Phifertex covers. Small piping—perhaps ⅛-inch cord—is generally preferable for cockpit cushions. A contrasting piping can give cushions a bit of extra pizzazz.

8 Starting at the zipper end, sew the boxing to one of the cover pieces with the piping sandwiched between. Leave about 2 inches of boxing and piping unstitched at your starting point. When you arrive there again, cut the boxing so it will overlap the end of the zipper by about an inch, allowing an extra ½ inch to turn the raw end under. Cut molded piping to abut. Cut covered piping to overlap about an inch, then snip the basting to open the piping, and cut the overlap amount off the cord. Turn about ½ inch of the piping fabric under and slip the starting end of the piping inside so that the cord now butts end to end. Be sure the finish end of the boxing is on the outside of the zipper assembly, then finish seaming the edge.

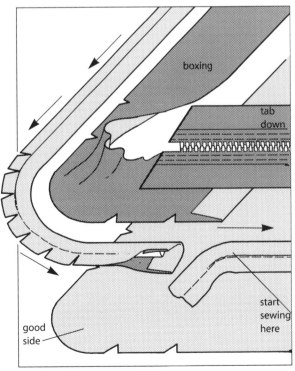

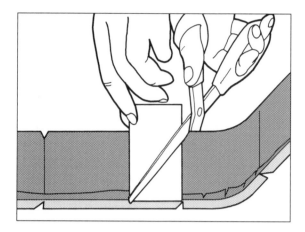

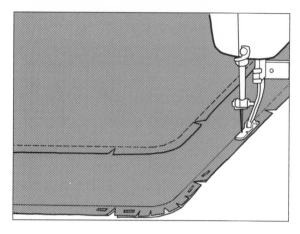

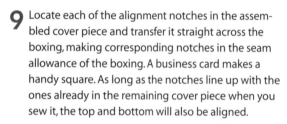

9 Locate each of the alignment notches in the assembled cover piece and transfer it straight across the boxing, making corresponding notches in the seam allowance of the boxing. A business card makes a handy square. As long as the notches line up with the ones already in the remaining cover piece when you sew it, the top and bottom will also be aligned.

10 Staple the second cover piece to the boxing with the notches aligned before you start sewing. This helps, but it doesn't prevent alignment problems, which can still arise as you sew around corners. Starting short of the separation in the boxing, sew the second cover to the boxing, watching the notches. If they get off more than $1/8$ inch, stop, take the last run of stitches out, and do it again. You can adjust the alignment somewhat by putting some tension on either the cover or the boxing as the machine drags it under the foot.

SEWING AROUND CORNERS

WHEN YOU GET TO THE CORNER OF A CUSHION COVER, you will get a better finished result if you round the corner slightly. Stop the machine—with the needle buried—an inch or so before the corner. Use your scissors to put two or three slashes in the seam allowance of the boxing and the piping where they will make the turn. Continue sewing until the needle is almost at the corner; then, with the needle again buried, rotate the material around the needle about 30 degrees. Turn the balance wheel by hand to make a single stitch, then rotate the bottom fabric an additional 30 degrees. Make one more hand-driven stitch, then rotate the fabric 30 degrees one more time. You want to end up with the needle $1/2$ inch from the new edge and the foot pointed in the right direction to continue sewing. With a little practice, that is just what will happen. Trim the extra material to the edge of the boxing before you turn the cover inside out.

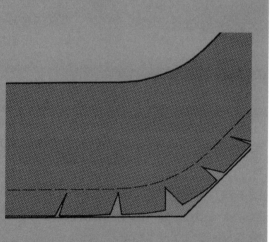

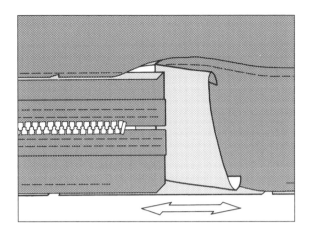

11 Leaving the two ends of the boxing open allows your stitching path around the second cover to be slightly shorter or longer than the first one. The length of the boxing will self-adjust; just make sure the end fold is perpendicular. It isn't necessary to stitch across this end unless it offends your sense of symmetry because of the stitching at the other end of the zipper.

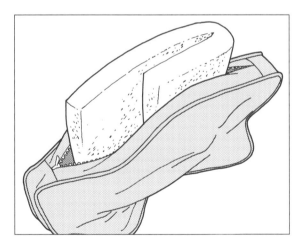

12 Unzip the cover and turn it rightside out, working the corners out with your fingers. Fold the foam and insert it into the cover, unfolding it inside. Try to limit the stress on the ends of the zipper. Work the foam until the corners are properly positioned, then close the zipper. Ta da!

KEEPING COCKPIT CUSHIONS IN PLACE

WHEN A SAILBOAT HEELS, cockpit cushions tend to slide off the seats. A short fiddle on the front edge of the seats will stop this, but unless the fiddle is removable, it will be an annoyance when the cushions aren't in place. The traditional way of securing cushions without a fiddle is with snap fasteners in a flap along the back of the cushion. Seam the ends of a lengthwise-folded strip of canvas and reverse it to put the seams inside. When you assemble the cover, sew this strip between the piping and the boxing on the bottom of the backside. For reversible cushions, put a matching flap in the top seam; the unused flap will lie flat behind the cushion when not in use. Install two or three snaps (or a strip of Velcro loop tape) in the flaps and attach their mates to the cockpit seat.

For an alternative that may be better because it doesn't take up space behind the cushion, you'll need two lengths of webbing, two boat snaps (small snaphooks), and two strap eyes. Thread the webbing through the boat snaps and box-stitch them to the boxing on either side so that the snaphooks just reach the back edge of the cushion. Install the strap eyes on the seat. Abutting cushions can attach to the same eyestrap. Center the webbing top to bottom for reversible cushions.

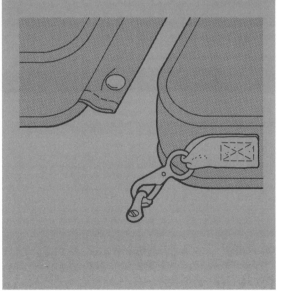

SETTEE UPHOLSTERY

Reupholstering loose below-deck cushions is exactly like covering cockpit cushions, with an occasional twist. For example, the top of a bunk cushion may be wider than the bottom to accommodate the flare of the hull, or a corner may be notched to fit around a removable "filler" cushion. And the style of the cushion may require a technique different from all-around boxing.

Some below-deck soft furniture may not be loose-cushion. For example, settee backrests often have a solid framework, typically a plywood back. Don't be put off by this; built-in backrests are often easier to cover than loose cushions.

FABRIC

Fabric choices for below-deck use are unlimited. Boat upholstery is likely to get wet occasionally—from an open hatch, a deck leak, or a wet bathing suit—so don't select a delicate fabric; but otherwise you can use any fabric suitable for your sofa at home. Keep in mind that bold patterns may require matching from cushion to cushion. Synthetics are more stain-resistant, but some tend to be hot, especially for sleeping. Fabrics intended for automotive upholstery can be especially durable in a boat. Vinyl bottom panels, commonly seen on factory cushions, have little to recommend them.

FOAM

Think about replacing the foam when you reupholster. Factory cushions are often too thin, and old foam goes soft. Choose polyurethane foam, not closed-cell EVA. Closed-cell foam tends to "deflate" over time as you sit or lie on it, becoming harder the deeper your shoulders and hips sink. Reinflation also takes time, so earlier depressions remain as you reposition, making for uncomfortable sleeping.

Polyurethane foam is rated by the weight required to compress it, but rating systems vary among manufacturers. You probably want 50- to 60-pound foam, but the best test is to put the piece on the floor and lie on it. Always err to the firm side. Don't buy "loaded" foam. Backrests, if they don't double as bunks, should be 25- to 35-pound foam.

As with closed-cell foam, cut polyurethane foam about $\frac{1}{2}$ inch oversize all around. Polyurethane foam doesn't shrink, but the extra foam will tighten the covers.

BEVELED CUSHIONS

Cushions lying against the hull may not have square sides. That causes the top and bottom pieces to have different dimensions, and the boxing on the beveled side will be wider than that on the square sides.

1 Outline the top and bottom pieces separately. Use the old cover or the foam as a pattern, adding a ½-inch seam allowance all around. If you have new foam cut ½-inch oversize, cut the fabric the same size as the foam.

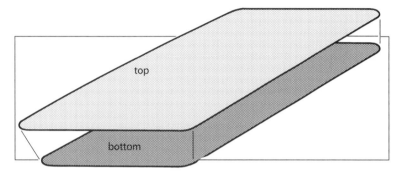

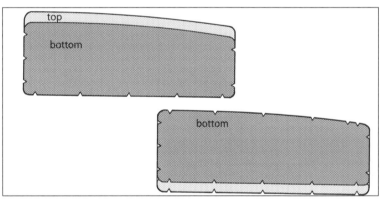

2 Alignment notches remain essential. With the two pieces good side to good side, align the three square edges and notch them in the seam allowance. Now slide the pieces to align the beveled edge and notch it.

3 Measure the width and length of the beveled edge on the foam and make your zipper assembly ¾ inch wider and 1 inch longer (see page 76). Cut the remaining boxing ¾ inch wider than the thickness of the foam and allow a couple of inches of extra length, being certain to get the length measurement from the larger of the cover pieces.

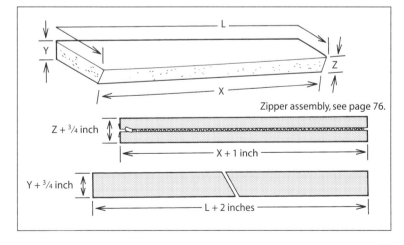

Zipper assembly, see page 76.

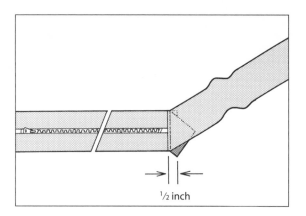

½ inch

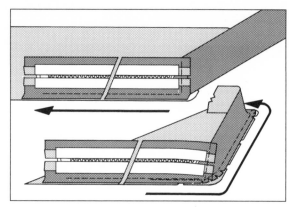

4 Fold one end of the boxing to match the bevel angle and sew it on top of one end of the zipper assembly, overlapping ½ inch. The length of the fold and the width of the zipper assembly should be the same. Trim the excess fabric.

5 This seam should align exactly with the intersection of straight side and the beveled side. To make that happen, place it about ⅛ inch shy of the corresponding corner on the larger of the cover pieces and sew back from it almost to the beginning of the zipper assembly (including piping if applicable). Now go back to where you started and sew in the opposite direction around the rest of the cover, stopping just short of completing the circuit.

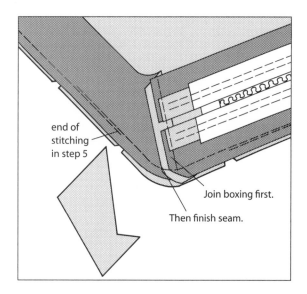

end of stitching in step 5

Join boxing first.

Then finish seam.

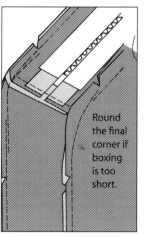

Round the final corner if boxing is too short.

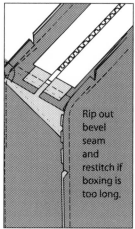

Rip out bevel seam and restitch if boxing is too long.

6 Fold the end of the boxing to match the bevel, locating the fold by estimating where it needs to be to end up precisely at the corner when you finish the seam. Sew the fold on top of the zipper assembly, overlapping a uniform ½ inch. Trim the excess boxing and finish the seam.

7 Transfer the alignment notches from the cover piece to the raw side of the boxing; then sew on the other cover piece starting from the zipper assembly. If you are diligent in keeping the pieces aligned, you shouldn't encounter any problems, but if the boxing runs slightly short, rounding the final corner to solve it won't matter. If it runs long, rip out the bevel seam and adjust it to fit.

BULL-NOSED CUSHIONS

Piping can be an irritant to bare legs, and twin hard ridges between cushions can be especially annoying when the settee is used as a bunk. Simply omitting the welt from a box cushion isn't very satisfactory. A better solution is the bull-nosed cushion.

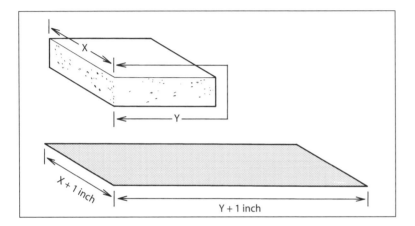

1 From the back edge of the foam, measure across the top, the front, and the bottom, and back again to the back edge and add 1 inch to get one dimension of the main piece of fabric. Add 1 inch to the width of the foam for the other dimension. The double width of the cover piece may be confusing, so pay close attention to the orientation of patterned fabric.

2 Measure the side dimensions of the foam and add 1 inch to both to get the side boxing. Two pieces are required. Use a compass to mark a perfect semicircle at one end and cut the boxing pieces to shape. Put alignment notches at the noon, 3 o'clock, and 6 o'clock positions.

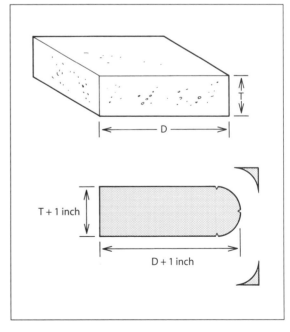

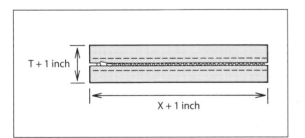

3 Make a zipper assembly 1 inch longer and wider than the foam's back dimensions (see page 76).

4 Fold the main piece in half and notch it at the fold on both sides. Unfold it and align one of these notches with the center (3 o'clock) notch of one of the boxing pieces. Sew from the notch to the back edge, running the machine by hand initially while you sew the curve of the boxing to the straight edge of the cover piece. Turn the assembly around and start again at the notch—overlapping a few stitches—to sew the other edge of the boxing to the cover.

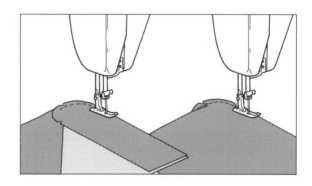

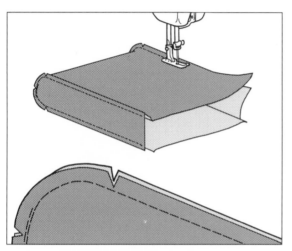

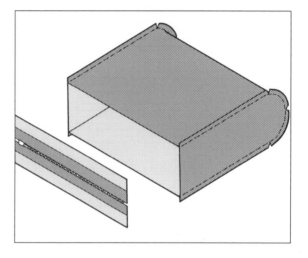

5 Transfer the noon and 6 o'clock notches across to the opposite edge of the cover with a square. Install the second piece of boxing the same way as the first, taking care to get the alignment right.

6 Trim the back edges of the cover to match the length of the side boxing, then staple the zipper assembly into the opening of the cover and seam it in place. Remove the staples. Open the zipper and turn the finished cover rightside out.

TRIMMING FOAM FOR BULL-NOSED CUSHIONS

TO GET A BULL-NOSED cushion to take the right shape, the front of the filling needs to be round. Rounding the foam requires special machinery, but you can approximate the rounded edge by putting five facets on the front edge. To hold the knife blade at 30 degrees, make the jig shown. Reversing the jig also allows it to hold the blade at 60 degrees. Make four cuts, then wrap the cushion with *polyester batting*.

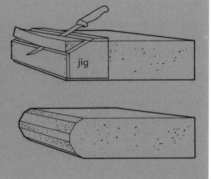

CENTER-WELT CUSHIONS

Center-welt cushions give an overstuffed look. They are most appropriate when at least two sides of the cushion will show. Center-welt cushions require a soft fabric, and the foam should be wrapped in batting.

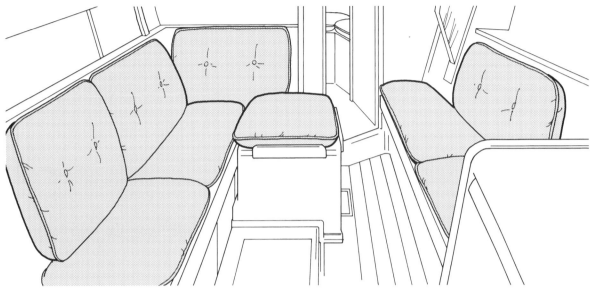

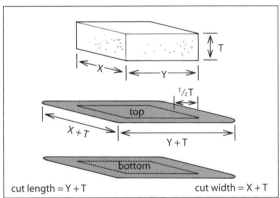

cut length = Y + T   cut width = X + T

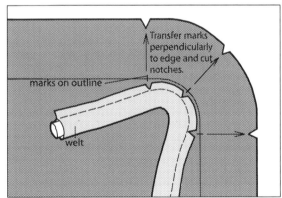

Transfer marks perpendicularly to edge and cut notches.

marks on outline

welt

1 Add the thickness of the foam to the length and width dimensions to get the cut size of the two pieces of fabric required. Round the corners. Draw an outline on the back side of the fabric half the thickness of the foam from the edge.

2 Thick welt is the usual choice for center-welt cushions. Put three evenly spaced notches in the welt so that when you shape the welt to the outline and put the center notch at the center of one of the rounded corners, the other two notches fall on the straight sides of the outline just beyond where the curvature of the corner starts. Use the notched cord to mark the outline with these three points at every corner.

3 Transfer these three points at each corner perpendicularly to the edge and notch their locations in the seam allowance. Replace the welt on the outline, aligning the initial three notches with the initial three marks; then align the welt all the way around the outline and notch it at the other nine marks on the outline.

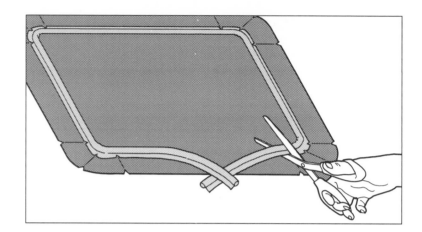

4 Fold the fabric back along the back edge of one of the cover pieces and sew it to a zipper so that the unsewn edge of the zipper replaces the raw edge of the fabric. Assemble the cover by sewing the welt around one cover piece, gathering the fabric at each corner to make the wide-spaced notches along the edge of the fabric align with the closer-spaced ones in the piping. Turn the assembly over and sew the second piece on the same way.

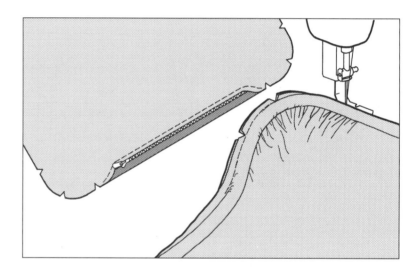

POLYESTER BATTING

IN ADDITION TO ROUNDING THE FRONT EDGE of a bull-nosed cushion, a layer of polyester batting, also called *wadding*, can give any style foam cushion some initial softness. Batting also tends to improve the cover fit. Polyester batting comes in a variety of weights; select a wadding about $1/2$ inch thick for wrapping cushions. Lay it on loose, or tack it in place with spray adhesive. If your foam will be batting wrapped, don't take the $1/4$ inch out of the boxing width measurements.

BACKRESTS

Built-in backrests are usually assembled on a thin backing of plywood. If they are self-contained, they are typically held in place with interlocking brackets. Try sliding the backrest straight up to free it. Otherwise, look for hidden fasteners.

A backrest can be unboxed or boxed on two, three, or four sides, depending on the cushion design. To get a perfect fit, always mark the fabric first where it should fold over the plywood.

Attach the fabric with closely spaced Monel staples installed diagonally, starting at the center of the top edge and working out in both directions at the same time. Do the bottom edge, then the sides the same way. Work the corners carefully, folding them under smoothly and gathering the fabric evenly if the backrest isn't boxed.

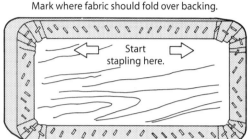

Mark where fabric should fold over backing.

Start stapling here.

BUTTON TUFTING

Tufting was once essential to hold cotton or hair padding in place. With solid foam padding, buttons are more decorative than functional, but they *can* keep backrest fabric from sagging.

The easiest and best way to get covered buttons is to take a piece of your fabric to an upholstery shop and let them press the buttons for you on a special machine. You can also cover your own using covered button forms from a dress shop, but these won't be quite as durable.

Mark the location of the buttons on the fabric and on the backing material of a backrest. Drill the backing. Fold a length of heavy waxed thread and run the folded end through the ring of a button, then open the fold and draw it over the top of the button to lock it. Thread both loose ends of the tie into a long needle and punch it through the mark in the fabric and out the drilled hole. Remove the needle and thread the ends through the two holes of a backer button. Pull the ends until the button is at the depth you want, then tie the ends together.

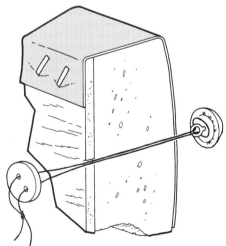

You can also button loose cushions in a similar manner, using a covered button on both sides. But keep in mind that buttoning prevents you from removing covers to clean them without cutting off the buttons.

PLEATED FABRIC

The pleated look, especially on a backrest, can be a nice design feature. The simplest route to the pleated look is to pleat the fabric beforehand, then construct the cushion in the normal way. Joining panels with diagonal pleats can create an interesting pattern.

You need extra fabric width—about ½ inch per pleat. Pleats can be any width, but 1 to 4 inches is normal. Mark your fabric *on the good side* with parallel lines spaced ½ inch farther apart than your desired pleat width.

Cut a piece of ¼-inch foam to the same size as your fabric and stitch it around the perimeter to the back side. You can also use polyester batting. Fold the fabric along your first pleat line and run a row of stitches ¼ inch inside the fold in the cloth. Because of the added bulk, the stitch line will be more than ¼ inch from the folded edge of the foam; to put the stitch line in the correct place, you'll have to experiment with how wide you want the seam to appear.

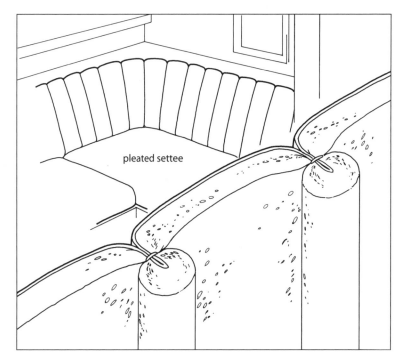

pleated settee

Continue folding and sewing until the entire piece is pleated, then cut the cover pieces you need from the pleated fabric. The finished cover may lie better if you have trimmed off the loop of foam or batting over the fabric folds.

CUSTOM UPHOLSTERY

Re-covering some items aboard, such as a navigator's seat, may require alternative techniques. The proper approach is to carefully remove the old cover, noting on a pad exactly how it is attached. The only new attachments you are likely to encounter are *tack strips* and *shaping flaps*. A tack strip is typically a flat strip of metal with tack-like barbs. The fabric wraps over the strip with the tacks protruding through the folded-under edge, then the covered strip is hammered into a wooden frame to yield a finished edge. Shaping flaps are usually just extra wide seams that are sewn or stapled down before fitting the cover completely to give the finished cover a concave shape.

With the cover removed, notch and label adjoining edges, then rip out the stitching and separate the cover into its component pieces. Use them as patterns for the new pieces—including the alignment notches—then simply reassemble and reinstall the cover the same way you took it apart.

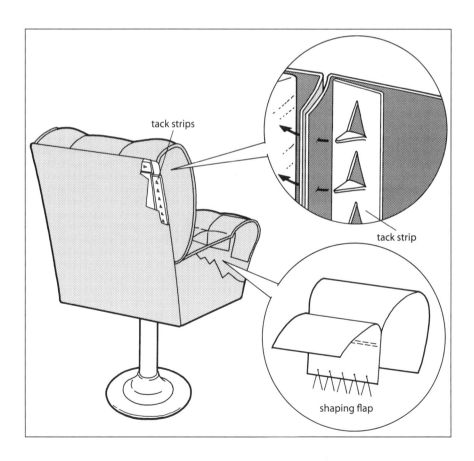

tack strips

tack strip

shaping flap

CUSTOM CANVAS

What if you want a sun cover for a sailboard? Is that much different from the zipper pockets we learned to make in "The Pocket"? Sew the folded edge to the contour of the board and trim away the excess canvas ½ inch beyond the stitch line. Contour the raw edges as well. The remaining steps are the same as for any zipper bag: Sew the raw edges to opposite sides of a full-length zipper, then seam and bind the ends.

How about a cover for the dink's outboard when it is rail-mounted? Nothing more than an appropriately sized bag with a drawstring or straps to secure it. (Give it handles and you will always have a tote bag in the dinghy.)

What about a secure way to get your cutlery to the beach for a picnic or cookout? Is what you need significantly different from a tool roll?

Most canvas items aboard a boat are some form of one of the four categories already covered, perhaps with a little shaping here, an extra seam there. Most, yes, but not all. A sailcover, for example, is more closely related to a sports jacket than a bag or a pocket. And a spray dodger may put you in mind of a convertible top for an old MG. Can the boatowner fabricate these odd-shaped canvas items? Of course.

If the project you have in mind is a replacement, the old item will serve as a pattern for each piece of fabric and as a guide to their assembly. Simply notch the seam allowances and label the pieces, then disassemble the item by ripping the seams. Lay the components on your new fabric—paying attention to the grain—and trace around them. Include the notches. Cut out the new pieces, then assemble them according to your notations.

If you don't have an old item to use as a pattern, then make one—using paper (or pattern fabric) and tape. Once you get the paper item to fit, cut it into pieces that will lie flat on your fabric—which generally means along the tape lines. Use a straightedge and a flexible batten when you trace the pattern to help you with the edges, and always remember to add seam and hem allowances as required. If your pattern fits, the item you make from it will also fit.

SAILCOVERS

Leave sails out continually in strong sunlight and they will be damaged in a single season, destroyed in three or four; but keep them covered and they will give a weekend sailor decades of use. Given that the cost of a sail is about 20 times that of a sailcover, it makes sense to have a cover and use it, and most sailors do. When the old one is faded or threadbare, making a new one is straightforward. Use acrylic canvas for all the usual reasons. Never make a sailcover from vinyl or any other fabric that doesn't "breathe."

1 If you don't have an old cover to use as a pattern, think of a sailcover as two wedge-shaped pieces of fabric seamed together on their longest edges, then lopped off on the pointed ends to let them wrap straight around both mast and boom. The distance from the front of the mast to the end of the boom gives the length of this truncated wedge. The height is measured from the bottom of the boom to a point about 6 inches above the dropped headboard. The seamed edge is usually concave to better match the contour of the furled sail; determine its exact shape by measuring from the bottom of the boom (and the front of the mast) to the center of the furled sail— around its bulk—taking measurements every 6 inches near the mast and every 2 feet once the curve flattens out.

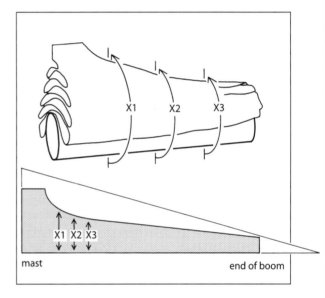

2 Add a ½-inch seam allowance to the curved side and a 6-inch fitting allowance to the boom end. Add 2 inches to all the other sides if you will close the cover with hooks and lacing, 4 inches if you plan to use twist fasteners. Lay out the two halves of the cover on the fabric. You can overlap the narrow ends to conserve fabric if both sides of the fabric are the same; if not, you must make the second piece the mirror image of the first. The fabric will probably be too narrow to accommodate the full height dimension of the cover; lay the excess out onto a paper extension, then transfer it back onto the fabric, allowing an extra inch of fabric along the edge that joins the main piece.

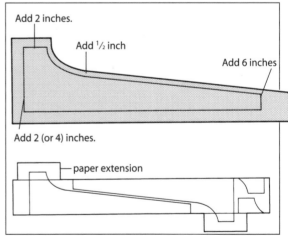

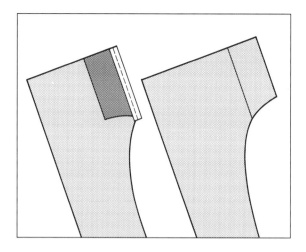

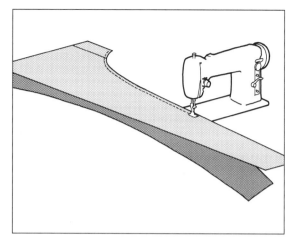

3 Sew the extension pieces to the main pieces with ½-inch seams. Bind these seams.

4 Sew the two cover halves together along the curve, good side to good side, placing the stitches ½ inch from the raw edges. Remove any pins or staples you used to baste the pieces together.

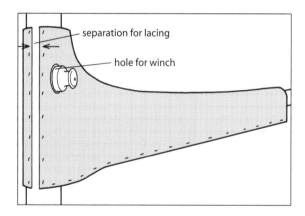

separation for lacing

hole for winch

5 Rub a 1½-inch (both folds) double-rubbed hem (see page 27) on the bottom and front edges and staple them to hold them temporarily. Place this cover "blank" over the sail and check it for fit. The edges should be a couple of inches apart for hook-and-lace fastening; for twist buttons they should overlap a couple of inches. Note any adjustments required. Mast-mounted winches may interfere with the fit; carefully position the cover and cut a hole in it to let the winch protrude. Also mark where you want the cover to end on the mast and boom and leave a 3-inch hem allowance.

6 After making all fit adjustments, bind the center seam. Open the two panels flat and fold the seam onto one of them, then sew it down with two parallel rows of topstitching. Trim the blank per your fitting marks and put a 1½-inch double-rubbed hem all around.

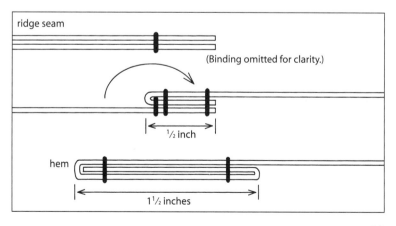

ridge seam

(Binding omitted for clarity.)

½ inch

hem

1½ inches

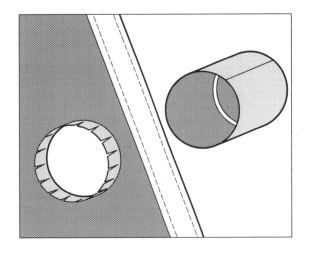

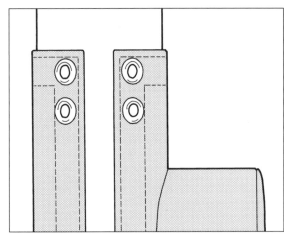

7 Cut a circle 2 inches larger than the winch hole and sew it inside an appropriately sized canvas tube to make a cover for the winch (see "Two-Piece Duffel," page 68). Turn this boot rightside out. Cut a series of ⅜-inch slits around the perimeter of the hole in the cover to allow the edge to fold in, then mate the raw edge of the boot with the edge of the hole and sew them together. Bind the seam.

8 Regardless of your closure system, install four grommets near the top of the front edges to allow the collar of the cover to be laced tightly against the mast. Having the collar tight prevents water penetration that leads to mildew. If the cover overlaps (for twist-lock fastening), set one pair of grommets back from the edge to allow tensioning.

9 For a hook-and-lace closure, install sailhooks on one side with a pair of grommets opposite. Place the hooks every 6 inches on the front of the mast, every 18 inches along the bottom of the boom. Hooks can be hand-sewn to the canvas or attached with pop rivets and washers. If you use pop rivets, be sure the proud side of the rivet is on the hook side of the cloth. Tie the lacing to the first pair of grommets (top and forward) and run it inside the cover, exiting the tandem grommets to capture the hook. Leaving the other end loose allows you to adjust the fit of the cover.

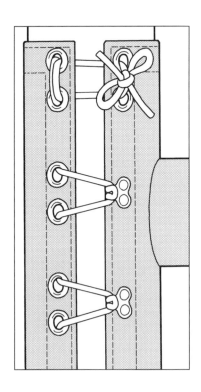

A SHORTCUT

SAILCOVERS DIE MOSTLY FROM HORIZONTAL EXPOSURE TO THE sun. If the hems that contain the hooks and grommets for closing the cover—around the boom and around the mast—are in good shape, save time and take advantage of the machine installation of the hardware by cutting off the old hems and seaming them to the edges of your new cover.

10 For a twist-button closure, install matching Common Sense studs and eyelets in the hems, using the same spacing as for the sailhooks above. Install them so that the fabric is overlapping, not pinched together. Use a heated knife to melt the slits for the prongs. Press the prongs through the slits and bend them with pliers over the appropriate backing plate. Cut the cloth from the center of the eyelet with a hotknife or a soldering iron *after* the eyelet is installed.

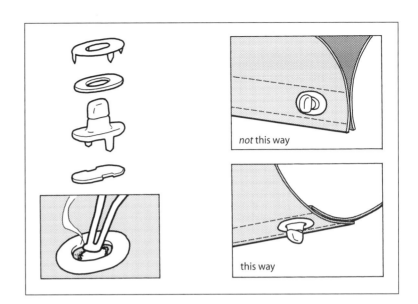

not this way

this way

11 Functionally it doesn't matter that a lace-on cover is slightly "open" on the front of the mast, but if you want a closed look, cut and hem a strip of canvas 4 inches wide and the same length as the height of the cover. Sew this flap to the inside of one side of the cover, or sew it to the outside and close it over the lacing with Velcro.

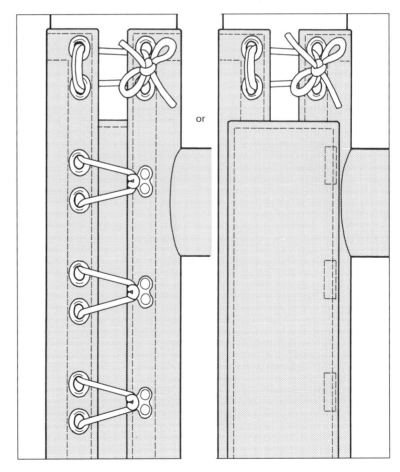

or

BOAT COVERS

In northern climes, a winter cover that keeps water off the deck prevents the damage caused when the water that has found its way into deck cracks freezes and expands. Storage covers are common, but boats *in use* are rarely covered despite the fact that the inconvenience of a cover may be more than offset by a significant reduction in maintenance. Covers are especially beneficial for varnished brightwork, but they also extend the life of caulking, plastic portlights, teak oil, covered hardware, and even surface gelcoat or paint; and they keep the decks clean and dry.

The waterproof and chafe-resistant nature of treated canvas makes it a good choice for a winter cover, but it must be kept clean to avoid mildew. It must also be stored clean and dry when not in use.

For regular in-season use, a light polyester fabric is sometimes selected because it makes a light, soft cover. Except for limited water-resistance, soft polyester (not sailcloth) isn't a bad choice if you don't mind replacing the cover every three or four years. Treated canvas is another possibility, but if you don't keep it clean, especially of bird droppings, mildew will quickly destroy it. For a carefree water-resistant cover that will last a decade or longer for in-season use, use acrylic canvas.

A day-use cover is basically a tarp—a flat sheet of canvas—shaped to the contour of the rail and pierced to let spars, wires, and other vertical features protrude. It can lie flat on the deck where it adds the least windage, or it can peak, tent-like, over the boom or some other support.

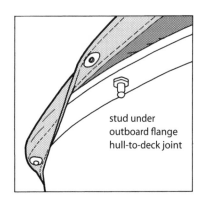

stud under outboard flange hull-to-deck joint

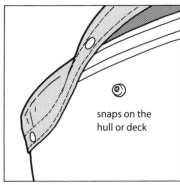

snaps on the hull or deck

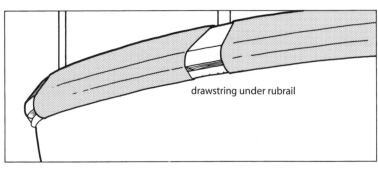

drawstring under rubrail

1 Start this project by deciding how the cover will be attached. This affects the amount of overhang all around and how the edges should be finished.

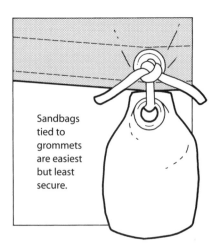

Sandbags tied to grommets are easiest but least secure.

2 Decide how the cover will fit around the mast. A zipper to one side is typical; making the cover in two parts is another choice. An overlap will be virtually watertight for a boat on a mooring, but if the boat can't clock to the wind, the overlap is likely to open.

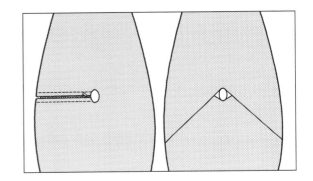

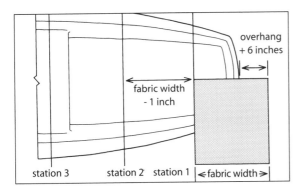

3 Starting at the stern, divide the boat into stations. The first station should be forward of the stern by the width of your cloth less 6 inches and the planned overhang. The remaining stations, all the way to the bow, should be 1 inch less than the width of your fabric apart. Measure them on the centerline of the boat if the cover will lie on deck, or along the ridgeline if the cover will be elevated over a support.

4 Begin construction by making up a blank—a piece of fabric roughly the size of your planned cover plus allowances for fitting. At the first station measure the distance from the centerline or ridgeline to the side rail and add to it the overhang plus 6 extra inches. Double this sum to get the length of the first panel. Make a similar measurement at the next station to get the length of the next panel. When you reach the longest station, cut two panels to that length—the length of a panel is determined by the longer of the two stations that border it. Continue measuring panel lengths all the way to the bow.

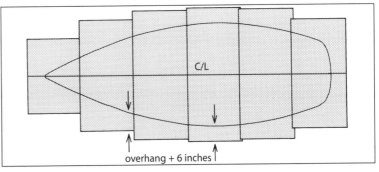

MILDEW LOVES THE DARK

THE BIGGEST PROBLEM WITH DAY-USE BOAT COVERS, aside from taking them off and putting them back on, is that they make the cabin dark. Add hot, humid weather into the mix and mildew quickly sets up housekeeping in your absence. The solution is open cutouts over transparent hatches. If that strategy lets more rain onto your deck than you think desirable, seal these openings with a clear vinyl window. The "Dodger" section at the end of this chapter contains instructions for installing vinyl windows.

5 Cut the panels and sew them together in the order you measured them, aligning their centerlines. Because the full-width panels have selvage edges (see page 40), a 1-inch overlap seam, triple zigzag stitched, is appropriate. Otherwise, use a flat-felled seam (see page 37).

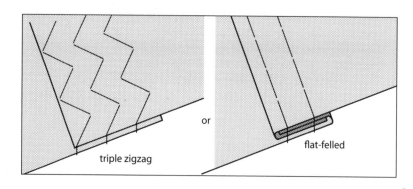

triple zigzag   or   flat-felled

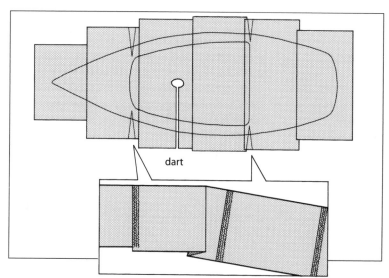

dart

6 Spread the blank on the boat so that it would overhang evenly all around if shrouds, stays, and stanchions weren't in the way. This requires making the mast cutout. Sew darts into the edge of the blank in line with slope changes on the centerline or ridge line to remove excess fabric at the rail. More extensive contouring to fit the cover to the shape of the cabin is generally unnecessary, but if you want to contour it, this is the time.

7 The cover will drape over low deck features, but cut holes for the windlass, cowl ventilators, and other features that interfere with the fit. Make boots (see "Sailcover") and sew them into the holes for the windlass and other protuberances you want covered. For a day-use cover, you may want ventilators to remain uncovered; in that case, bind the edge of the holes.

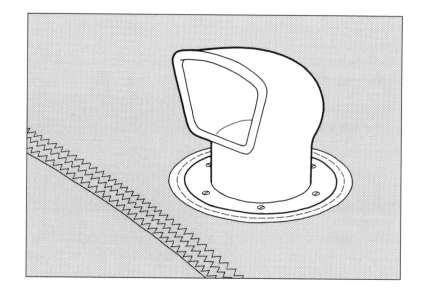

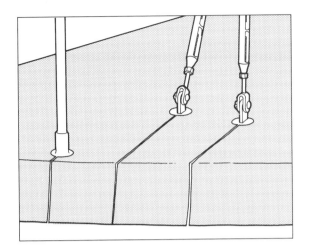

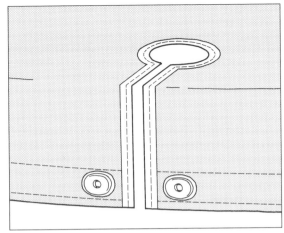

8 Working from the dock or a dinghy and taking care that the centerline of the blank remains aligned with the centerline of the boat, make a cutout for every penetrating feature at or near the rail. Slit the blank from each cutout to the edge. Mark the perimeter of the finished cover, accounting for your fastening system.

9 Add an appropriate hem allowance and trim the edge. Bind the raw edges of all the cutouts and slits. Hem the perimeter of the cover and install the planned fasteners.

TAILORING

A COVER THAT LIES ON DECK WILL HAVE A NEATER appearance if it is tailored to the contour of the forward end of the trunk cabin. Cut the blank straight across, using the deck corners of the cabin to position the cut. Cut three paper patterns, one for the outline of the cabin on the deck, one for the outline of the forward edge of the cabintop and sides, and one duplicating the front surface of the cabin. Taped together these three patterns should neatly enclose the forward end of the cabin. Mark them on the centerline.

   Cut the forward section of the blank to the deck-contour pattern, and the aft section to the cabin contour pattern, adding ¾-inch seam allowances. Cut an additional piece of canvas the shape of your front-surface pattern, also with ¾-inch allowances. Seam the three pieces together with ½-inch flat-felled seams.

   Use the same technique to tailor your cover to accommodate a doghouse or any other deck contours.

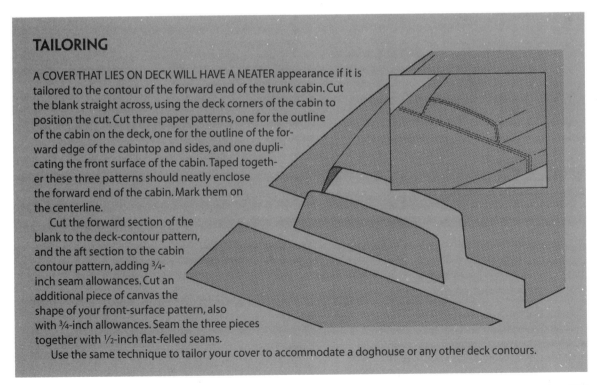

BIMINI AWNING

A Bimini awning is another flat-sheet project, hemmed on the sides and given casings on the ends shaped to the contour of the supporting frame. Because the frame adjusts to the cloth, a perfect fit requires only reasonably accurate end

contours. Reinforced vinyl and acrylic canvas make good Bimini tops. Acrylic canvas will need to be sprayed with a proof coating every couple of years to keep water from penetrating.

THE FRAME

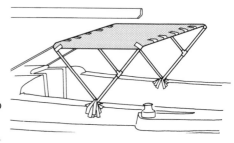

1 If you're starting from scratch, you need a frame for the top. Make a mock-up from plastic water pipe and elbow fittings. Cover it with Kraft paper or pieces of old bed sheet, then sail with it. Does it interfere with the mainsheet? Does the boom clear? Can you get to the jib winches? Can you go forward easily? Can you see to trim the sails? Will the top fold out of the way? Work out the problems you discover.

BENDER

nailed to base
1 x 2
2 x 4
nailed to lever
radius at least 12 inches
³/₄-inch plywood
pivot bolt
washers between

2 Aluminum tubing is a common frame material, but it distorts easily. Stainless steel tubing is a better choice although heavier and more expensive. Steel tubing should be ⁷/₈ or 1 inch (OD) with a wall thickness of 0.049 or 0.065 inch. Bend the bows on a bender fashioned from ³/₄-inch plywood. Make the radius at least 12 inches to avoid flattening or kinking. Making the bends short of 90 degrees so that the width between the ends prior to mounting is 8 or 10 inches wider than the distance between the mounting sockets will introduce curvature to the top when you install the bows, strengthening the frame and improving water shedding.

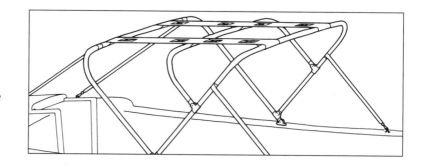

3 Install the frame and space the bows with webbing with loops sewn in the ends, and in the middle if you have intermediate bows. Position and install (temporarily) the tie-down straps.

THE PATTERN

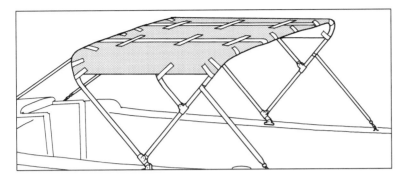

1 If you are making a replacement top, take apart the old top as a pattern. For a new top, cover the spread frame with paper or pattern material taped tightly around the bows.

2 Mark the pattern material along the forwardmost edge of the forward bow and the aftmost edge aft. Decide how far down the sides you want the top to reach and mark both sides fore and aft. Mark the locations of the tie-down straps. If the frame has intermediate bows, trace them along both sides on the underside of the pattern.

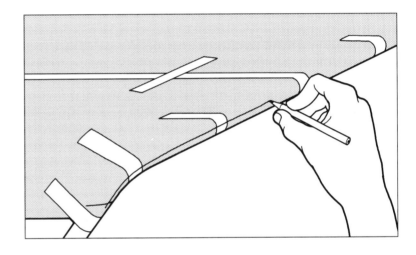

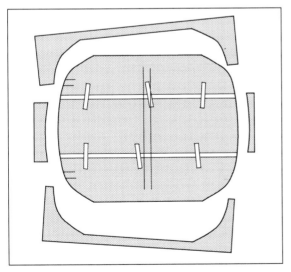

3 Remove the pattern material. Connect the side marks with straight lines, then cut out the pattern.

THE TOP

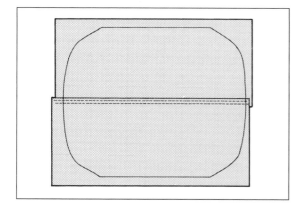

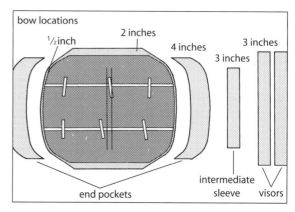

1 Sew two or more panels together—as required—to make a blank large enough to accommodate your pattern. The seam(s) should run fore and aft. With an odd number of seams, put the center seam in the center of the top. With an even number, place the center panel at the top's center. Sew the panels together with flat-felled seams.

2 Trace the pattern onto your fabric, adding a ½-inch allowance to the ends and a 2-inch allowance to the sides. Mark the intermediate bow location(s). Cut out two end-pocket pieces about 4 inches wide (including allowances) that exactly match the contour of the ends of the top piece but 3 inches shorter. Sleeves for intermediate bows are straight strips about 3 inches wide and two-thirds the top's width. Cut two 3-inch-wide visor strips 3 inches shorter than the curved ends of the top piece.

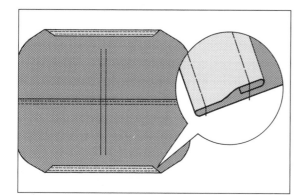

3 Put a 1½-inch double-rubbed hem (½ inch turned under) on both sides of the top.

4 Mark the location of the tie-down straps on the end-pocket pieces and make arched cutouts. Hem or bind the cutouts. Hem the ends and the concave side of the end pockets, and the ends and one side of the center pocket(s).

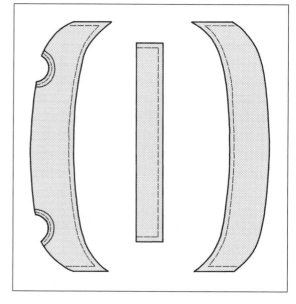

5 Fold the visor strips in half lengthwise—good side inside—and seam the ends ½ inch from the edge. Reverse the fold to put the seams inside. Align the raw edges and sew the top and the end pockets together— good side to good side— with the visor strip between them.

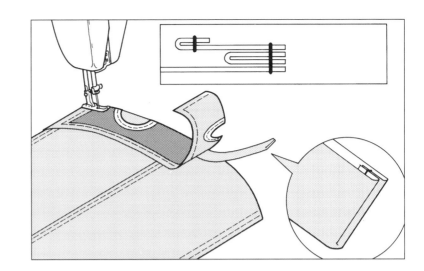

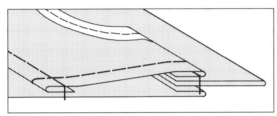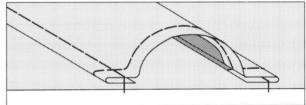

6 Fold the end pockets over and press the seam flat, then sew the hemmed side (not the ends) to the top piece. Sew the raw edge of the intermediate pocket(s) to the underside of the top along one of the marks then fold it over and sew the hemmed edge along the other mark. If you want your top removable without dismantling the frame, attach the hemmed edges of the pockets with jacket zippers rather than sewing them.

7 Install the Bimini by sliding the loose bows through the appropriate sleeves. Remember to install the stitched loops of the tie-down straps at the sleeve cutouts as you insert the bows. Mount the bows and adjust the straps.

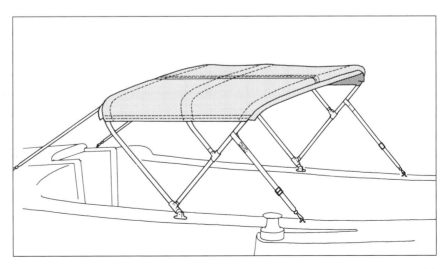

DODGER

It may be helpful to think of a dodger as a short Bimini awning (preceding project) with a windshield and side curtains. The frame is basically the same as a two-bow Bimini frame. Aluminum tubing is *not* appropriate for a dodger frame; the rigidity of stainless steel is essential. For the best visibility, use 0.020 polished sheet vinyl for the windshield.

DESIGN

1 As with the Bimini, making a water-pipe mock-up is a smart first step. Can you easily enter and exit the companionway? Does the boom clear? The winch handles? How will the lower edge of the windshield cross the companionway slide? Can you stand at the helm and see *over* the dodger when the windshield is salt-fogged? Get off the boat: Does the dodger look too short? Too high? Too boxy? Windshield too vertical?

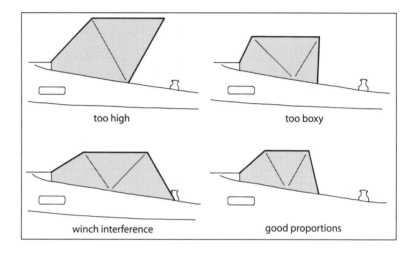

too high

too boxy

winch interference

good proportions

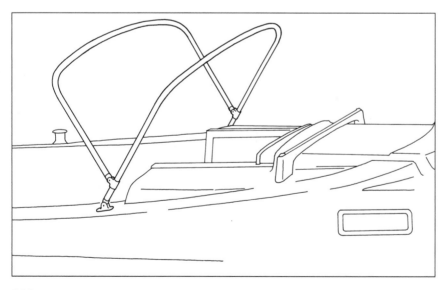

2 Bend the bows and install the frame (see "Bimini Awning— The Frame," step 2). A large radius gives the dodger a rounded look that on many boats is more pleasing. Underbend the bows slightly to make the ends wider apart than their sockets, which introduces curvature to the center of the bow when you mount it.

3 Cover the mounted and guyed frame with paper or pattern fabric. Work all wrinkles out of the pattern material. Tape a separate piece of pattern fabric to the forward bow and to the deck to represent the windshield portion of the dodger. Add "wings" to close the sides of the dodger. Draw in the outlines of clear panels for the windshield and side ports. Mark seam locations.

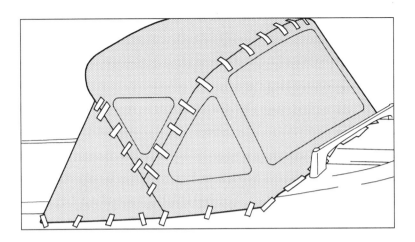

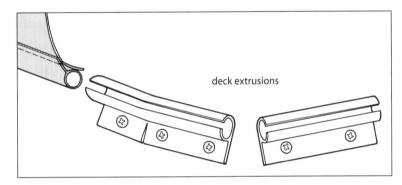

deck extrusions

4 Work out all attachment issues. The most waterproof method of attachment is a boltrope in the edge of the dodger that slides through a deck-fastened extrusion. Cutting the mounting flange allows the extrusion to be bent moderately; for more radical turns, install the extrusion in sections. Alternatively, attach the front edge with turn buttons and the sides with snap fasteners. Snaps won't work on the front edge because the upward pull will unsnap them. The wings typically have a corner grommet for a lacing.

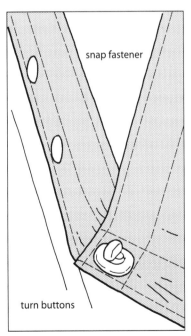

snap fastener

turn buttons

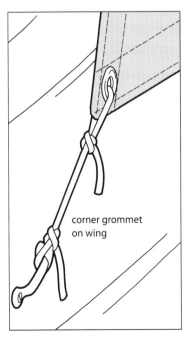

corner grommet on wing

ASSEMBLY

1 Cut the pattern apart on the seam lines. Cut the top piece from your fabric, remembering to add a ½-inch seam allowance. Also cut the wing pieces, giving them an extra 1½-inch allowance for a wide hem on the two free sides. Cut grommet-reinforcement corner patches (two) for each wing and install them under the hems.

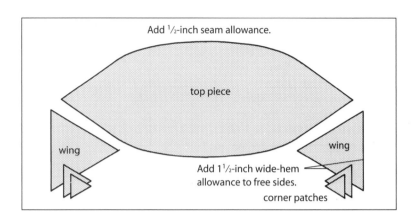

2 The windshield is typically divided into three pieces joined with zippers, which allows you to open the center panel for ventilation. The easiest way to fabricate the windshield section is to frame the vinyl pieces with hemmed canvas strips. Folded strips give a finished appearance inside and out, and they make the vinyl easier to sew. Always use your longest stitch on vinyl. Place zippers on the inside of the windshield and oriented to unzip up.

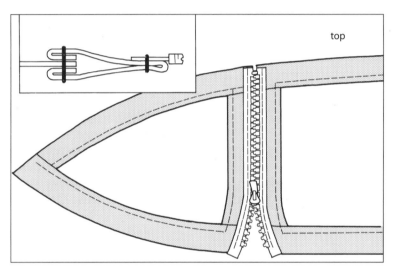

3 Cut two 4-inch-wide sleeve pieces to match the forward and aft contours of the top piece. The forward sleeve need only be 3 or 4 feet long: it simply holds the forward bow in position. Make the back sleeve long enough to extend about halfway through the side curves of the bow. Hem the ends and concave sides. If you want the dodger to be easily removable, sew #10 jacket zippers to the hemmed sides.

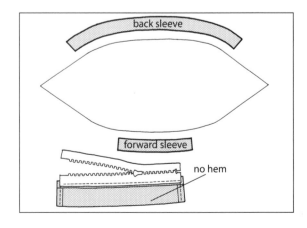

4 A dodger quickly becomes your preferred handhold. Cut a 3-inch-wide strip of leather or reinforced vinyl to protect the aft edge of the dodger.

5 Install the clear side ports. Cut the vinyl 1 inch larger than the finish size on all sides, and sew it to the inside surface of the top piece in the appropriate location. Cover the vinyl with Saran Wrap to keep the foot of your sewing machine from sticking. Cut the canvas 1 inch inside the stitch line. Do not make this cutout *before* you sew the vinyl in place. Make a regular series of ³/₈-inch slits in the curved portions of the cut edge, then fold ¹/₂ inch under and topstitch it down.

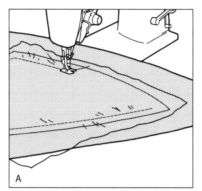

A

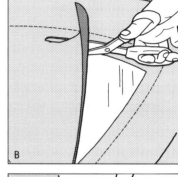

B

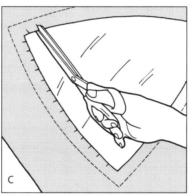

C

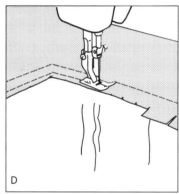

D

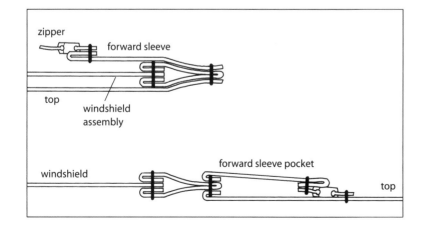

zipper
forward sleeve
top
windshield assembly
windshield
forward sleeve pocket
top

6 Sew the top, the windshield assembly, and the forward sleeve together, sewing in both directions from the centerline to assure proper alignment. Fold the pocket piece under, pressing the seam flat, and sew the pocket's aft edge or its zipper to the top.

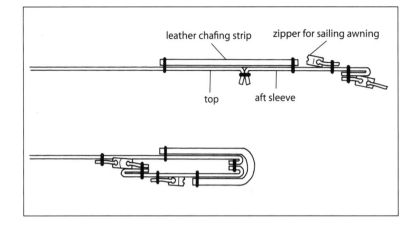

leather chafing strip   zipper for sailing awning

top   aft sleeve

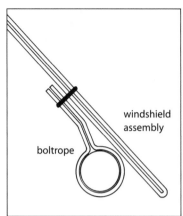

windshield assembly

boltrope

7 Sew the top, the aft sleeve, and the wings together. Where the wings and sleeve overlap, be sure the wing piece is in the middle. Open the seam flat and sew the leather chafing strip to both the sleeve and the top. If you plan to have a sailing awning that attaches to the dodger, now is also the time to sew on the dodger half of the jacket zipper. Fold the sleeve under, pressing the seam flat, and sew its aft edge or its zipper to the top.

8 Install the dodger on the frame and mark the locations for the fasteners. Remove the dodger and install appropriate fasteners in it. Install grommets in the reinforced corners of the wings. If you are using bolt rope, sew the rope inside a canvas strip or binding tape (similar to piping—see page 79), then sew the tape to the inside of the bottom edge of the windshield assembly.

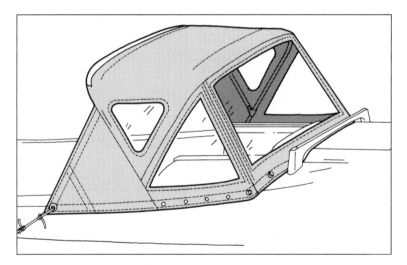

9 Reinstall the dodger and guy the aft bow in position. Mark the deck for the boltrope extrusion and/or the deck half of the various fasteners. Working from the center out in both directions, smooth the top and install and fasten each fastener in turn to get even tension on the canvas. Install strap eyes below and behind the wing grommets and use a lacing to tension the installed dodger.

SAILING AWNING

YOU CAN QUICKLY CONSTRUCT A SIMPLE SAILING AWNING for your dodger from an appropriately sized flat sheet of canvas. Put a casing in one end and hem the remaining three edges. Insert a stiff batten into the casing and sew half of a jacket zipper to the other end. Zip the zipper to its mate (see step 7 above on page 114), tie the batten to the backstay, and sail in the shade.

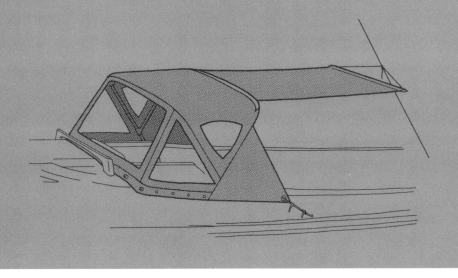

SAIL REPAIR

The most significant canvas item on a sailboat is the sail. Is it advisable, or even possible, to apply your new or improved canvasworking skills to sail repair?

Consider this. The most basic canvas item, as we have already seen, is a flat sheet with edges hemmed and grommets installed in the corners. The difference between a lee cloth and a harbor awning is mostly a matter of scale, plus the addition of perimeter features like corner reinforcement and perhaps a rope in the hem. Start with a triangular sheet of fabric and you end up with something that looks an awful lot like a sail.

Wait a minute! Sails aren't flat. Neither are awnings or lee cloths when they're doing their job. Okay, it is true that most sails have built-in shape, a certain amount of fullness behind the luff, but by now you know how to introduce such fullness—even if you don't know that you know. Remember the hatch cover in "The Bag"—a flat piece of canvas with darts in the four corners? Dart just two corners and you end up with fullness behind one edge—just like a sail.

Anyway, the fullness doesn't matter for repairs to the sail's perimeter, and since "shape" is almost always confined to the forward third of the sail, the aft two thirds *is* flat. Besides that, every panel of cloth is flat, so repairs confined to a single panel have no effect on sail shape.

Restitching a sail, however, can be significantly more challenging than other flat-sheet projects for two reasons: fabric and size.

Dacron sailcloth, especially new cloth, is stiff and slick. While softer fabrics adjust to hide minor sewing indiscretions, sailcloth is as unforgiving as plywood. Even the slightest misalignment shows up as a pucker or a wrinkle, and the fabric is so slippery that pinching two pieces together is like squeezing a wet bar of soap. Fortunately there is a simple solution: When sewing sailcloth, glue every seam together before you sew it. Transfer tape or a glue stick make this easy.

The complications of size are not quite as easily overcome. Size is of little consequence for repairs near the edge, but finding a way to get the presser foot into the middle of a 500-square-foot sail can be a real challenge. It is possible that your sail may be too big or your machine's underarm space too small to meet this challenge, but you won't know unless you try. Aside from size, sail repair is just another flat-sheet project.

UNDERSTANDING SAIL SHAPE

Sails aren't really flat, and it is a good idea to understand what gives them shape so you don't unwittingly change it. Some high-tech racing sails have the shape "molded" into the sail, but all others are shaped by some combination of two basic techniques.

LUFF ROUND

If you round the leading edge—the *luff*—of a sail, straightening it when you hoist the sail moves excess fabric back into the sail. This gives the sail fullness behind the luff. Luff round alone was adequate to shape cotton sails, but the stiffness of resin-impregnated Dacron tends to restrict the effectiveness of this technique. Dacron sails are still given rounded luffs, but a second technique is required to move the draft back from the luff.

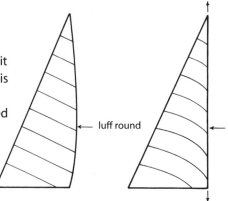

BROADSEAMING

Broadseaming is nothing more than increasing the overlap of two panels as you seam them together toward the edge. It works much like a dart, removing cloth from the edge of the sail. This results in more cloth in the center of the sail than at the edge. This bagginess gives the finished sail its draft and is controlled by where the broadseams begin and how much the overlap increases.

LEECH HOLLOW

The aft edge—the *leech*—of unbattened sails is typically given a concave contour. This is not to shape the sail but rather to tighten the edge to keep it from fluttering. The amount of hollow is typically about 2 percent of the length of the leech, but varies according to the intended use of the sail. The leech may also be tightened with a broadseam or two at the aft edge of the sail.

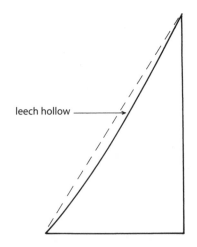

leech hollow

Ben Franklin was onto something with that "stitch in time" thing. Almost every sail problem begins with a single broken thread. Spot a problem early and you significantly limit the extent of the repair required.

TAPE

The easiest way to close a seam or tear is with fabric tape. Special sail-repair tapes in 2- or 3-inch widths are available, and the better ones will last a season when properly applied. Duct tape, although unsightly, also does an admirable job. Place the damaged section on a flat surface and clean both sides with an alcohol-dampened cloth to remove oils and displace moisture. Apply the tape to both sides of the sail, extending it well beyond the damage. Press the patch with a roller or pound it with a mallet or a shoe. Tape also makes excellent chafe patches.

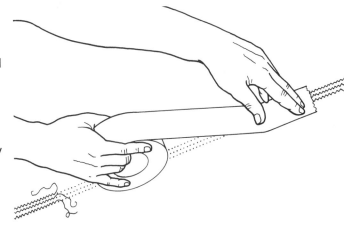

GLUE

Contact cement is another way to quickly patch a large tear or a split seam. Some glues permanently stain sailcloth, but in an emergency a stained seam may be a minor concern. Coat the sail and the patch, or both surfaces of an open seam. Keep the two parts apart while the adhesive dries tack-free, then carefully align the two sides and press them together. Such a repair will be quite strong. If you don't have sailcloth aboard, you can cut a patch from some canvas item or an old foul-weather jacket. The glue in your inflatable repair kit is contact cement.

HAND-SEWING

The best way to repair a tear or split is to sew a patch in place or restitch the seam, but hand-sewing, if there is much of it, is slow and tedious. For general-purpose sail repair, select a #16 needle with a triangular shank. Use waxed polyester sail twine. A sewing palm will make the work much easier.

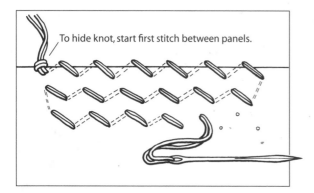

To hide knot, start first stitch between panels.

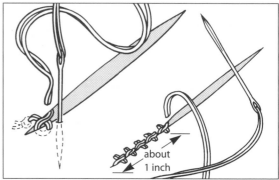

about 1 inch

1 Hand-sew split seams and loose tabling (edge binding) by passing the needle through the original holes. This assures correct alignment. If the split is in the middle of the sail, the repair goes much quicker with a person on both sides of the sail feeding the needle back and forth. The finished job looks like a row of slanted stitches. The twine is much stronger than machine thread, so there is little reason to fill the other side of the zigzag.

2 Repair tears in the fabric with a herringbone stitch, also called a *sailmaker's darn*. Knot the end of the doubled twine to start the repair. Make four or five stitches per inch and place them well back from the edges. Pull the stitches tight enough to bring the torn edges together, but not so tight that you introduce a pucker. Tie off and tuck the loose end.

USING A SAILMAKER'S PALM

HOLD THE THREADED NEEDLE between your thumb and forefinger and seat the eye end into the dimpled metal guard. Stick the point of the needle into the cloth, then release your grip on the needle and push it straight through with the palm. It is important, especially when sewing through several layers, not to let the needle get out of column or you may break it. You will quickly learn to feel when your palm pressure is directly down the center of the needle. When most of the needle has been pushed through the cloth, grip it again and pull it the rest of the way. Reseat it in the metal guard and you are ready for the next stitch.

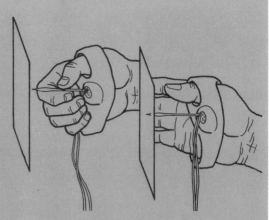

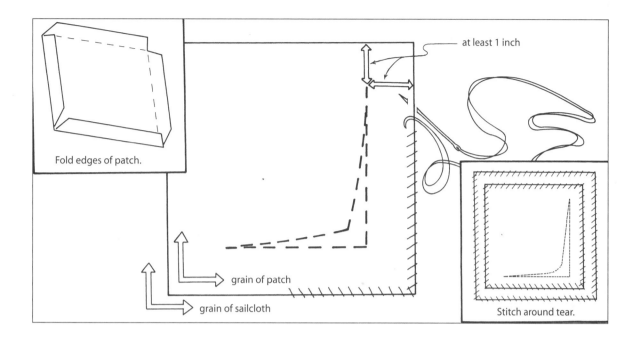

Fold edges of patch.

at least 1 inch

grain of patch

grain of sailcloth

Stitch around tear.

3 Sew repair or chafe patches to the sail with a flat seaming stitch. Always align the grain of a patch with the grain of the sail. Sewing around a patch is easier if you pin or glue it in place. Adhesive-backed sail tape or sailcloth is ideal for sewn patches. Seal or fold the edges of plain sailcloth. Sew with the patch on top, pushing the needle down through the sail, then back up through the sail and patch in one motion. Pull each stitch snug before making the next one. Place a second row of stitches around the tear.

REPAIR KIT

NO MATTER HOW WELL YOU MAINTAIN your sails, splits and tears are an ever-present possibility. Brand-new racing sails have been holed by the wadding from the starting cannon. Just a few sail-repair items aboard can save the day. Start your kit with a roll of sail-repair tape. Inexpensive nylon "ripstop" is adequate for weekend repairs, but for offshore sailing put stronger and stickier adhesive-backed Dacron tape in your kit.

Your kit should include a dozen or so triangular sailmaker's needles in sizes #16 and #14 and a cone of prewaxed sail twine. If you have a spinnaker aboard, throw in a package of heavy domestic needles and a tube of heavy polyester thread. A leather palm is essential for pushing a thick needle through multiple layers of sailcloth. Also include a small pair of scissors, a seam ripper, and a block of beeswax.

In addition to the tape, it is a good idea to have a couple of yards of Dacron sailcloth aboard. A piece of leather will also be handy for chafe patches. Throw in a couple of jib hanks and a couple of sail slides with their attendant hardware, and you are ready for most contingencies.

EXAMINING YOUR SAILS

The best way to catch that first broken stitch is to carefully examine your sails at least once a year—more often if they see daily use. Don't be afraid to tug at a seam if it looks suspect; now is the time to find out if it is about to let go.

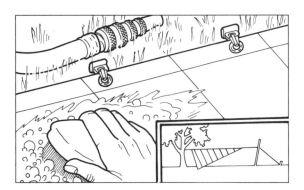

1 Washing the sail first is a good idea. Spread it on the lawn and scrub it with a soft brush and a mild detergent, then rinse thoroughly. Wash the opposite side. Hang the sail by the head and tack to let it dry. Never machine-wash a sail! Forget about trying to remove stains; any chemicals strong enough to succeed are also likely to damage either the fabric or the resin.

2 Spread the sail on the lawn, remove your shoes, then crawl all over the sail dragging your finger over *every* seam. This forces you to look at every stitch. Mark every problem with a single tied stitch of brightly colored thread; pencil marks are too easily overlooked, and a strip of tape can peel off. You can use a pencil *in addition to* the thread flag to outline the extent of the needed repair.

3 Check each of the batten pockets. Battens often chafe against the inside of the pocket. Holding the sail up to the light may reveal thinning fabric.

4 Check the headboard for loose rivets or worn stitching. Check the tack and clew for chafe and problems with eye or ring installations. Check the leech for wear. Examine boltropes or their casings. Check the attachment of every hank or slide.

RESTITCHING SEAMS

By far the most common sail repair is restitching. Stitches stand proud on the hard sailcloth and are the first thing damaged when the sail chafes. Thread also weakens with exposure and age.

1 For Dacron sailcloth, use a #18 or larger needle in your machine. Most stitch problems you are likely to encounter can be solved by increasing the needle size. Set the stitch length to the maximum, then adjust the zigzag width to sew a "square" pattern—each stitch about 90 degrees to the previous one. Sailcloth is too hard for the interlock between upper and lower threads to pull into the fabric, so when the upper tension is right, the threads will form a tight knot on the underside at each stitch.

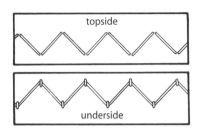
topside

underside

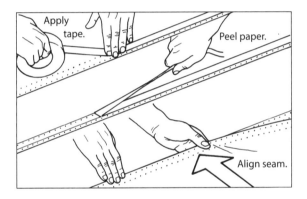
Apply tape.
Peel paper.
Align seam.

2 Baste the seam together. If some of the old stitching is still in place, leave it to maintain the alignment of the panels. If the panels are separated, use seam tape to rejoin them, carefully aligning the old stitch holes as you stick the panel edges together. You can also align and baste the panels with long hand stitches through corresponding stitch holes.

3 Sewing a sail is often easier if you get the machine down on the floor so you don't have to lift the sail. Sit in the lotus position and operate the foot pedal with your knee. You can handle short repairs alone, but a helper will make restitching long splits much easier.

4 Roll the sail like a scroll and feed it under the foot of your machine. Clamp the ends of the rolls or put tight lashings on the sail after it is under the foot to keep the roll diameters small. Stitch along the edge of the top panel, placing one side of the zigzag stitch just off the edge. Slide the sail out and turn it over to put the bottom panel on top. Sew along its edge. Finish the repair with a third row of stitches between the first two.

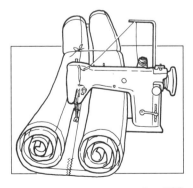

You are hoisting away when the belly of the sail finds the end of an unprotected cotter pin. It happens. As long as you can get the sail under the arm of your machine, repairing a tear is not very difficult, and except for a small visual reminder of your indiscretion, the sail will be none the worse for the incident. If the tear crosses a seam, patch each panel independently, then sew them back together

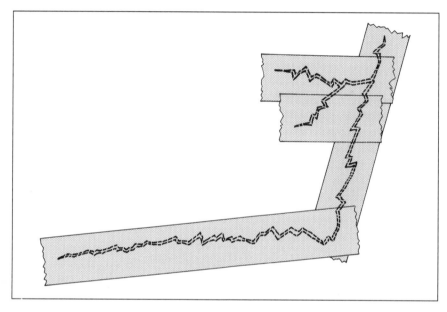

1 Spread the torn portion of the sail over a flat surface and realign all the torn edges. Take great care to get the cloth back into its original alignment. Tape the tear closed. Almost any tape will do. Don't let the tape extend far beyond the tear.

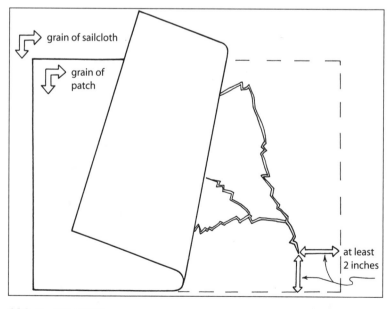

grain of sailcloth

grain of patch

at least 2 inches

2 Use a soldering iron or a hotknife to cut a rectangular patch of sailcloth similar in weight to the sail. Make the patch large enough to overlap the tear by at least 2 inches, keeping in mind that the grain of the patch must match the grain of the panel. Use seam tape or a glue stick to attach the patch to the sail on the side opposite the tape.

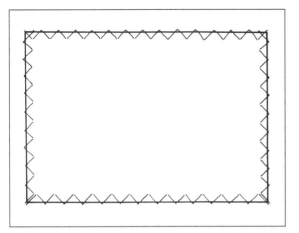

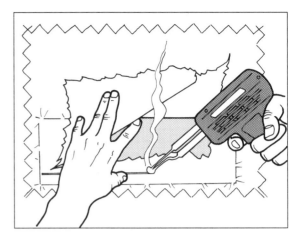

3 Stitch around the perimeter of the patch with a square zigzag stitch.

4 Turn the sail over and peel the tape. Slide a shield between the sail and the patch (through the tear) and carefully use a hotknife to cut the sail 1 inch inside the patch stitching.

USING A HOTKNIFE

WHENEVER POSSIBLE, CUT synthetic sailcloth with a hotknife. This seals the edges so that a hem is generally unnecessary, making the sail smoother and reducing weight. The usual hot knife is nothing more than a common soldering gun with a special "burning" tip that looks like a flat vertical disk. Placing a smooth, heat-resistant surface—such as a ceramic tile—under the cloth will help make your cuts easy and uniform.

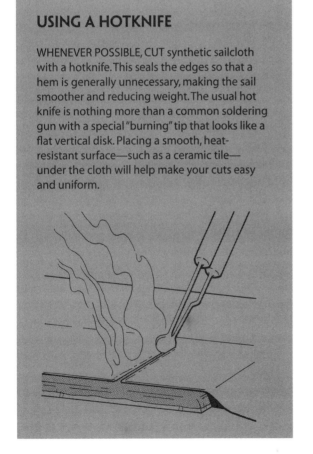

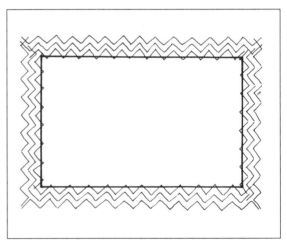

5 Sew around the edges of the rectangular hole. Add a third row of stitches between the first two.

REPLACING PANELS

Sometimes the damage is so severe or the cloth so weak that replacing a section of a panel is a better alternative. This can be simple or complicated, depending on where the panel is and how much needs to be replaced. You need sailcloth of approximately the same weight as the original.

1 Decide how much of the panel you want to replace. The job will be significantly easier if the replacement doesn't involve the edge of the sail. With a pencil, trace onto both adjoining panels the edge of the section you are replacing. Use a framing square to mark cut lines across the panel perpendicular to the edges.

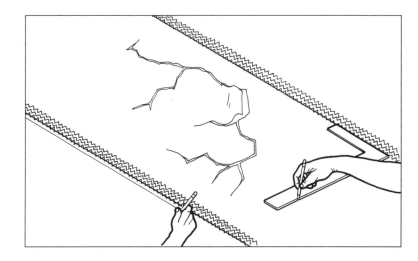

2 Hotknife the replacement panel 2 inches longer than the distance between your two cross-panel lines. Place the new panel on the old one and see how closely their widths match. The standard sailcloth width is more or less 36 inches. If they match perfectly, the side lines you traced will be an accurate guide. If the new panel is wider, measure the difference and move one of the edge lines out that distance. If the new panel is narrower, note the difference so you can move a guideline in after you remove the old panel.

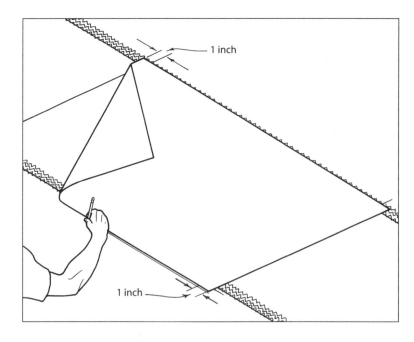

1 inch

1 inch

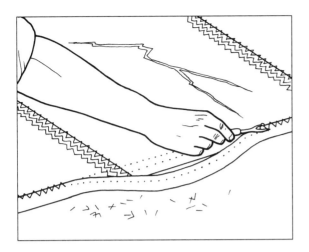

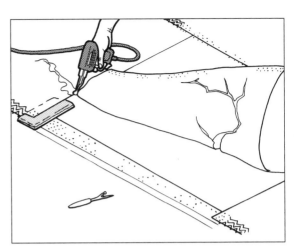

3 If the replacement extends to the edge of the sail, use a seam ripper to unstitch any casing, tabling, or hems that cross the panel.

4 Rip the panel seams, opening them a couple of inches beyond the cross-panel pencil lines. Use a hotknife to cut the panel on the lines, taking care not to touch the adjacent panels with the knife.

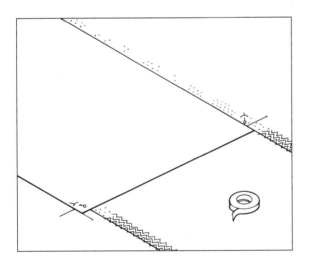

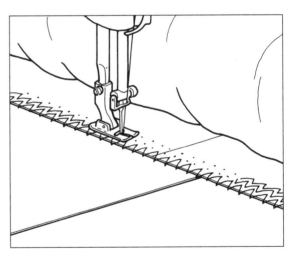

5 Redraw the guidelines if necessary, then glue the new panel into position with seam tape or a glue stick, taking great care to align the edges perfectly with the guidelines. The replacement panel should evenly overlap the sail 1 inch at each end (unless it extends to the sail's edge). Use pins or staples to reinforce the adhesive at the corners of the replacement.

6 Roll the sail (if necessary) and sew one edge of the replacement panel. Start and finish the stitching far enough beyond the panel to reseam the sections not removed. Put in all three rows of stitches.

7 Unroll the sail and seam one end of the replacement.

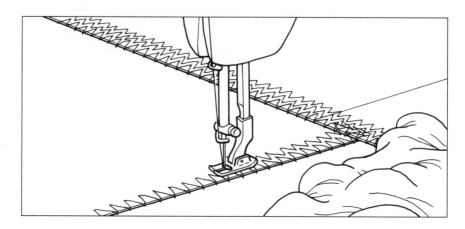

8 Lay the sail flat and make sure the unsewn edge is properly aligned with your guideline. Roll the sail again and seam this edge.

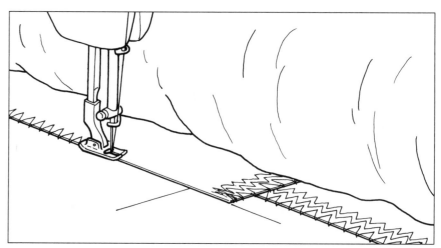

9 Seam the end of the panel or, if it extends to the edge of the sail, use the old panel as a pattern to trim it to the appropriate contour. Hem the edge or reattach the loose tabling or casing.

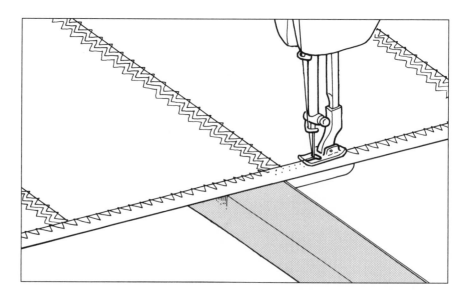

BATTEN POCKET REPAIRS

Battens chafe inside their pockets. Worn stitching is easy enough to repair. Damage to the cloth is somewhat more difficult, but easier than panel replacement because all the sewing is near an edge of the sail.

SPLIT POCKET OPENING

Repair the leech end of batten pockets by hand-sewing the seams with waxed sail twine. The twine resists the chafe of the batten better than machine thread. Use a round stitch—five stitches per inch—to close and/or reinforce the end seam. Put a couple of stitches at the top of the pocket opening.

TORN CLOTH

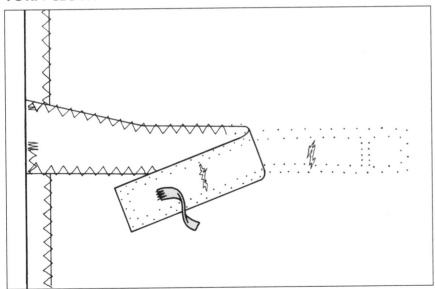

1 Rip the seams to release the pocket at the damaged end. To make an effective repair, partially separate the pocket from the sail; if you don't, the aft edge of a patch will close the pocket. If the pocket has an elastic tensioner, unstitch it from the sail.

2 Repair sail damage with a patch on the opposite side of the sail from the pocket. This avoids creating an edge inside the pocket that can catch the batten. For the same reason, rather than cutting out the damage (see "Patching a Tear" above), reduce the length of your square zigzag by about half and sew over the torn or worn spot to capture it.

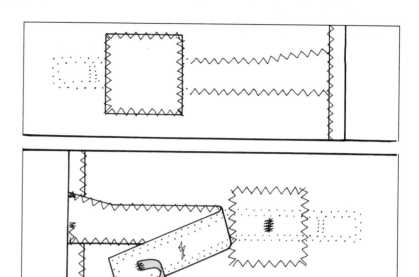

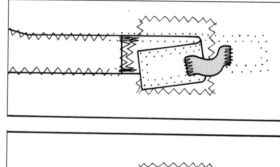

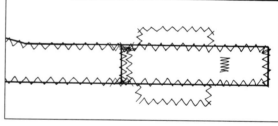

3 Repair pocket damage by cutting off the damaged end and replacing it. To avoid an edge inside the pocket, sew the new piece on top of the old one.

4 Restitch the elastic tensioner, then glue the edges of the pocket to the sail and sew them back down.

CHAFE PROTECTION

Avoid damage to your sail with strategically located chafe patches. Likely locations are where the mainsail bears against the spreaders off the wind and where the foot of a genoa rubs the pulpit or lifelines.

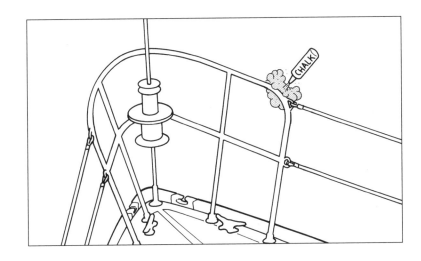

1 Mark the outside limits of the chafing area. Powdered chalk can help.

2 With a hotknife, cut matching sailcloth patches for both sides of the sail. Be sure the grain of the patch will match the grain of the sail where it will be applied. Make the patches a couple of inches larger than the protected area to avoid subjecting the stitching to chafe. Use seam tape to apply one patch, then glue the second in place on the opposite side, aligning it to the first. Sew down the edges of both patches at the same time.

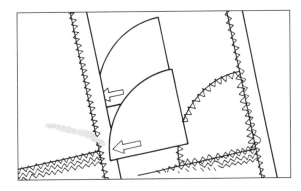

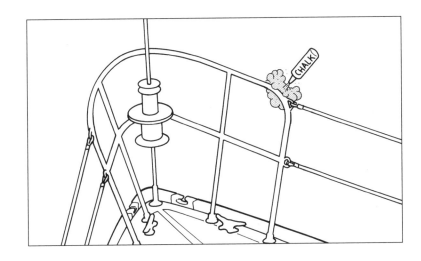

3 Use leather for edge protection. Make edge patches large enough to fold around the edge and protect both sides.

CLEW DAMAGE

Heavy loads at the clew can distort and even tear a sail. Rebuilding the clew with additional corner patches may exceed the capacity of a domestic sewing machine, but you can still effect a strong and long-lasting repair. Cut three 18-inch lengths of 1-inch webbing and pass them through the eye or D-ring. Pull them tight against the forward edge of the ring and hand-sew them to the sail—one along the foot, one along the leech, and one midway between the other two. Make long zigzag stitches to minimize perforation. Protect the webbing with a leather butterfly if needed. Use the same technique to reinforce leech cringles and the tack.

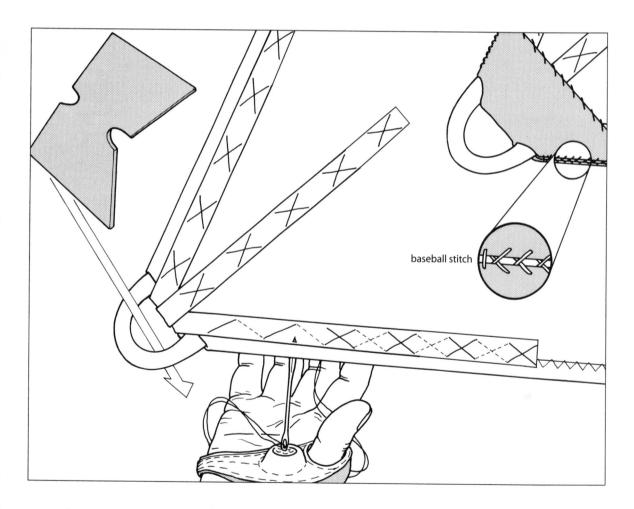

baseball stitch

LEECH LINES

Like shoestrings, leech lines break, and tying them back together just doesn't work. Replacing a leech line is easy. The best leech line is braided Dacron, often sold as flag halyard. The most common size is ⅛ inch, but light sails are often built with 1/16-inch line.

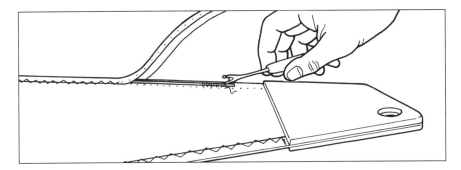

1 Rip the leech tabling seam at the head of the sail to expose the end of the line. It is usually sewn down, so cut the stitches to release it.

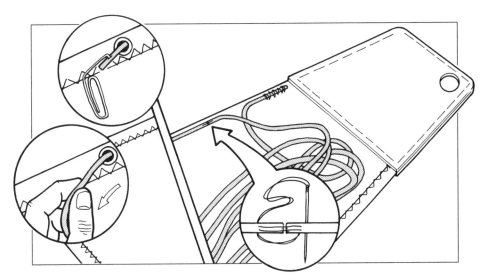

2 If the line broke at the eyelet near the clew—the usual spot—you can save some effort by fishing out the end with a straightened paper clip with a small hook bent on the end. Sew a new length of the same diameter line to the top of the sail, then attach its loose end to the old line with a couple of loops of thread sewn through the lines. Pull the new line through the tabling with the old one.

3 If the old line broke inside the sail, pull the remaining piece out from the top. Sew on a new line. Cut a 10-inch length of coat-hanger wire and round one end with a file. Nick the wire near the other end. Make a couple of stitches through the line, then tie the thread to the wire at the nick. Use a push-pull action to thread the wire through the tabling and out the bottom eyelet.

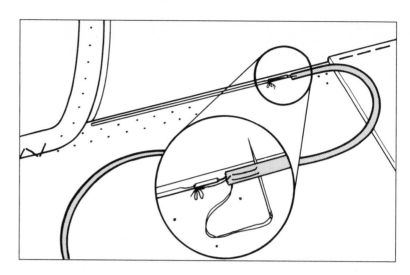

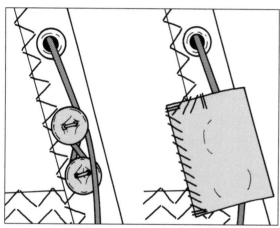

4 Restitch the tabling at the top of the sail. A pair of buttons cut from stiff leather make leech-line adjustment easy. Add them if your sail doesn't have them. On a headsail protect the buttons from snagging on shrouds with a stiff covering flap sewn only along its top and forward edges.

HANKS AND SLIDES

Plastic slides break and the lashings that hold hanks to the sail chafe through. Hanks and slides can be attached in a number of ways. You are most likely to reattach a hank or slide the way it was originally, but if a hank or slide attachment is a recurring problem, consider one of the alternative attachment methods shown.

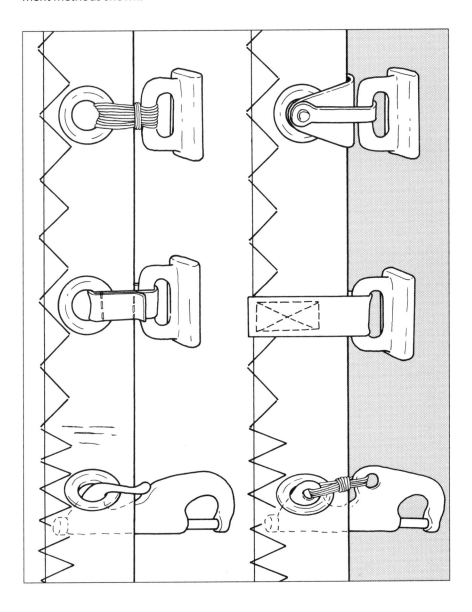

GLOSSARY

along the grain (of fabric): parallel to the threads. See page 29.

back-sew: the process of locking stitches by sewing backward over a few stitches at the start and finish of a row. See page 26.

bind: to finish an edge with a narrow strip of vinyl or cloth tape folded and sewn over raw fabric, eliminating the excessive bulk of a hem. See page 52.

box-stitch: a four-sided stitching pattern, usually enclosing an X joining opposite corners. See pages 48 and 85.

boxing: the strip of cloth that joins the top and bottom of a cushion. See page 82.

broadseaming: increasing the overlap of two (sail) panels as they are seamed to introduce fullness. See page 118.

butterfly: to spread the raw edges of a seam to place equal bulk on either side. See page 79.

casing: essentially a double-rubbed hem without the row of stitching near the outermost edge; usu-

ally used to contain a drawstring or elastic. See page 58.

dart: a triangular pleat. See pages 33 and 66.

double-rubbed hem (or double hem): the result of twice folding, rubbing a crease in, and stitching a raw edge to yield a finished edge. See page 27 for a full description and illustration.

flat-felled seam: a seam concealing raw fabric edges within the fold of the fabric; used when both sides of the fabric will be visible in a finished project. See page 37 for a full description and illustration.

hotknife: a cutting tool that seals fabric edges as it cuts; a common soldering gun with a special "burning" tip. See page 125.

mitering: a process by which a less-bulky hemmed corner can be constructed. See page 46 for instructions.

on the bias (of fabric): diagonal to the thread lines. See page 29.

overlap seam: a seam formed by overlapping the

edge of one piece of fabric on top of the edge of the second piece and stitching them together; generally used to join panels with selvaged edges. See page 40.

overcast: to capture the loose threads of a raw edge by placing one side of a zigzag stitch just beyond the edge. See page 35.

piping: a bead of fabric used to hide stitching and provide exposed seams with a finished look. See page 79 for instructions.

pleat: a fold in cloth made by doubling material over on itself and stitching into place. See pages 59 and 94.

sailmaker's darn: herringbone stitch. See page 120.

selvage: the finished edge on the sides of cloth when it comes from the weaver. See page 40.

tabling: the binding at the edge of a sail. See page 127.

tack strip: a metal strip with barbs; used to create finished edges when upholstering items with wooden frames (such as a chair). See page 95.

topstitch: to make a line of stitching on the outside of an item. See page 99.

transfer tape: tape that leaves only the adhesive behind when the paper is removed; useful for holding pieces in place before sewing. See page 11.

wadding: batting; a fibrous matting used to give cushions softness and improve cover fit. See page 92.

warp: yarns running lengthwise in fabric. See page 29.

weft (or fill): yarns running across fabric. See page 29.

welt cord: see piping.

INDEX

A

Acrylic canvas, 13
Appliqué, 35
Awnings
    Bimini, 4, 106–110
    harbor, 42–49
    sailing, 115

B

Backrests, 93
Bags, 63–73
    multi-pocket bags, 60–61
    rigid bottoms for, 65
    sheet bags, 58–59
    tote bags, 64
    two-piece duffel bags, 68
    zippered duffel bags, 78–80
Batten pocket repairs, 129–130
    split pocket openings, 129
    torn cloth, 129–130
Battens for dive flags, 39
Batting, 92
Bimini awnings, 4, 106–110
    frame, 106
    pattern, 107
    top, 108–109
Binding, 52
Boat covers, 102–105
    tailoring, 105
Bobbins, 11
    tension, 20
    winding, 19
Bolsters, 76–77
Box-shaped projects
    closed, 75–95
    life-jacket, 72–73

Boxing, 82
Broadseaming, 118
Button tufting, 93

C

Canvas
    acrylic, 13
    custom, 97–115
    treated, 13
Canvaswork, reasons to do yourself, 4–5
Chafe protection, 131
Circles, drawing, 68
Clear vinyl, 14
    pockets, 54
    windows, 103
Clew damage, 132
Closed canvas boxes, 75–95
Cloth. See also Fabric
    batten pocket repairs, 129–130
    Dacron sailcloth, 117
    lee cloths, 29–30
    terry cloth liners, 28
    weather cloths, 31–35
Cockpit cushions, 81–85
    keeping in place, 85
Colors, 15
Corners
    mitering, 36
    sewing around, 84
Covers
    boat covers, 102–105
    drawstring, 67
    hatch covers, 66–67
    sailcovers, 4, 98–101
    snap-on, 66–67
    winch covers, 70–71

Curtains, 49
Curves, hemming, 32–33
Cushion corners, sewing around, 84
Cushions
    beveled, 87–88
    bull-nosed, 88–92
    center-welt, 91–92
    cockpit, 81–85
Custom canvas, 97–115
Custom upholstery, 95
Cutouts, 103
    hemming, 32–33
Cutting tools, 10

D

Dacron, 14
    sailcloth, 117
Dive flags, 38
    support batten for, 39
Dodgers, 31, 110–114
    assembly, 112–114
    design, 110–111
    sailing awning for, 115
Double hems, 27
Drawing circles, 68
Drawstring covers, 67
Duffel bags
    two-piece, 68
    zippered, 78–80

E

Eyestraps, 85

F

Fabric, 13–15, 86
    colors and patterns, 15

pleated, 94
selecting, 52
upholstery, 15
Fasteners, snap, 16, 85
Fender skirts, 26–28
    terry cloth liners for, 28
Finishing tools, 11
First aid, 119–122
Flags, 36–38
    diver's flag, 38
    Q flag, 36–37
    support battens for, 39
Flaps, shaping, 95
Flat-sheet projects, 25–49
Foam, 17, 86
    trimming, 90
Foot pressure, 21
Frames, 106

G
Glue, 119
Grommets, 11, 16
    installing, 28

H
Hand-sewing, 120–121
Hanging storage pockets, 52–54
Hanks, 135
Harbor awnings, 42–49
    design, 42
    external spreaders, 48
    measuring, 43
    panels, 45
    side curtains, 49
Hatch covers, 66–67
    drawstring, 67
    snap-on, 66–67
Hemmed corners, mitering, 36
Hemming
    curves and cutouts, 32–33
    double, 27
Hook and loop tape (Velcro), 17
Hotknife, 11, 125

J
Jacket zippers, 77

K
Knots, trucker's hitch, 31

L
Leather linings, 57
Lee cloths, 29–30
    fabricating, 30
    installing, 30

measuring and cutting, 29
Leech lines, 133–134
Life-jacket boxes, 72–73
Linings
    leather, 57
    terry cloth, 28

M
Marking tools, 10
Measuring tape, 10
Mildew, 103
Mitering hemmed corners, 46
Multi-pocket bags, 60–61

N
Needles, 11
    broken, 21
    buying, 12
Nylon, 15
Nylon ripstop, 121

P
Panels
    making, 45
    replacing, 126–128
Patch pockets, 64
Patching tears, 124–125
Patterns, 15
    Bimini, 107
Pencils, 10
Piping, 79–80
Pockets, 35, 51–61
    batten pockets, 129–130
    clear pockets, 54
    closures for, 54
    hanging storage pockets, 52–54
    making, 53
    multi-pocket bags, 60–61
    patch pockets, 64
    split openings, 129
    tool rolls, 56–57
    zipper pockets, 55
Polyester (Dacron), 14
    batting, 92
    bonded, 12
    sailcloth, 117

Q
Q flags, 36–37

R
Repair kit, 121
Restitching seams, 123
Rippers, 11
Ripstop, 121

S
Sail repair, 117–135
    batten pocket repairs, 129–130
    broadseaming, 118
    clew damage, 132
    first aid, 119–122
    hand-sewing, 120–121
    hanks and slides, 135
    leech lines, 133–134
    patching tears, 124–125
    replacing panels, 126–128
    restitching seams, 123
    tears, 129–130
Sail repair kit, 121
Sail shape, 118
Sailcloth, 117
Sailcovers, 4, 98–101
    shortcuts, 100
Sailing awnings, 115
Sailmaker's darn, 120
Sailmaker's palm, 120
Sails
    chafe protection for, 131
    examining, 122
    leech hollow, 118
    luff round, 118
Scissors, 10
Seam rippers, 11
Seams
    broadseaming, 118
    flat-felled, 37
    restitching, 123
Settee upholstery, 86
Sewing
    around corners, 84
    double hem, 27
    by hand, 120–121
    tools for, 11
Sewing machines, 8–9
    bobbin tension, 20
    features and adjustments, 8
    foot pressure, 21
    getting ready to use, 18–21
    locking stitches, 26
    oiling, 18
    problems, 22–23
    pulling thread from cone, 18
    selecting, 9
    stitch length, 20
    threading, 19
    upper-thread tension, 21
Sheet bags, 58–59
Side curtains, 49
Signal flags, 36–38
Slides, 135

Snap fasteners, 16, 85
Snap-on covers, 66–67
Soldering iron, 11
Split pocket openings, 129
Spray dodgers, 31
Spreaders, external, 48
Stitch length, 20
Stitches
    locking, 26
    puckered, 22
    restitching seams, 123
    sailmaker's darn, 120
    skipped, 23
    uneven, 23
Storage pockets, hanging, 52–54
Supplies, 7–21
Support battens, 39

T

Tack strips, 95
Tailoring boat covers, 105
Tape, 119
    measuring tape, 10
    transfer tape, 11
    Velcro, 17
    zipper tape, 77
Tears
    batten pocket repairs, 129–130
    patching, 124–125
Terry cloth liners, 28
Thread, 12
    buying, 12
    pulling from cone, 18
Tool rolls, 56–57
Tools, 10–12
    for cutting, 10
    for finishing, 11
    for marking, 10
    for sewing, 11
Tote bags, 64
Transfer tape, 11
Treated canvas, 13
Trucker's hitch, 31
Tufting, button, 93

U

Ultraviolet (UV) radiation, 4
Upholstery
    custom, 95
    settee, 86
Upholstery fabrics, 15
UV radiation. *See* Ultraviolet (UV)
  radiation

V

Velcro, 17
Vinyl
    clear, 14
    open-weave, 14
    reinforced, 14
Vinyl pockets, 54
Vinyl windows, 103

W

Wadding, 92
Weather cloths, 31–35
    installing, 34
    pockets on, 35
    putting letters on, 35
Welt cord, 79
Winch covers, 70–71
Windows, clear vinyl, 103
Windscoop, 39–41
Wings, 111

Y

Yardsticks, 10

Z

Zipper foot, 11
Zipper pockets, 55
Zipper tape, 77
Zippered duffel bags, 78–80
Zippers, 17
    jacket, 77
Z-twist, 12

International Marine/
Ragged Mountain Press

A Division of The McGraw·Hill Companies

Published by International Marine

10   9   8   7   6

Library of Congress Cataloging-in-Publication Data
Casey, Don.
Canvaswork and sail repair / Don Casey.
    p. cm. — (The International Marine sailboat library)
    ISBN 0-07-133391-3
    1. Marine canvas work. 2. Sails—Maintenance and repair.
    I. Title. II. Series.
    VM531.C36 1996
    623.8'62—dc20   96-206
                                         CIP

Questions regarding the content of this book should be addressed to:

International Marine
P.O. Box 220
Camden, ME 04843

Questions regarding the ordering of this book should be addressed to:

The McGraw-Hill Companies
Customer Service Department
P.O. Box 547
Blacklick, OH 43004
Retail customers: 1-800-262-4729
Bookstores: 1-800-722-4726

Canvaswork & Sail Repair is printed on 60-pound Renew Opaque Vellum, an acid-free paper that contains 50 percent recycled waste paper (preconsumer) and 10 percent postconsumer waste paper.

Illustrations in Chapters 1, 3, and 7 by Rob Groves.
Ilustrations in Chapters 2,4, 5, and 6 by Jim Sollers.
Printed by R.R. Donnelley, Crawfordsville, IN.
Design and layout by Ann Aspell.
Production by Molly Mulhern and Mary Ann Hensel.
Edited by Jonathan Eaton, Ann Greenleaf, and Tom McCarthy.

Front Cover Photo by William Thuss.

DON CASEY credits the around-the-world-voyage of Robin Lee Graham, featured in *National Geographic* in the late sixties, with opening his eyes to the world beyond the shoreline. After graduating from the University of Texas he moved to south Florida, where he began to spend virtually all his leisure time messing about in boats.

In 1983 he abandoned a career in banking to devote more time to cruising and writing. His work combining these two passions soon began to appear in many popular sailing and boating magazines. In 1986 he co-authored *Sensible Cruising: The Thoreau Approach*, an immediate best-seller and the book responsible for pushing many would-be cruisers over the horizon. He is also author of *This Old Boat*, a universally praised guide that has led thousands of boatowners through the process of turning a rundown production boat into a first-class yacht, and of *Sailboat Refinishing* and *Sailboat Hull & Deck Repair*, part of the International Marine Sailboat Library. He continues to evaluate old and new products and methods, often trying them on his own 27-year-old, much-modified, Allied Seawind.

When not writing or off cruising, he can be found sailing on Florida's Biscayne Bay.

THE INTERNATIONAL MARINE SAILBOAT LIBRARY

Canvaswork & Sail Repair has company:

Sailboat Refinishing
by Don Casey
Hardcover, 144 pages, 350 illustrations, $21.95. Item No. 013225-9

Sailboat Hull & Deck Repair
by Don Casey
Hardcover, 144 pages, 350 illustrations, $21.95. Item No. 013369-7

The Sailor's Assistant: Reference Data for Maintenance, Repair, and Cruising
by John Vigor
Hardcover, 176 pages, 182 illustrations, $21.95. Item No. 067476-0

Inspecting the Aging Sailboat
by Don Casey
Hardcover, 144 pages, 350 illustrations, $21.95. Item No. 013394-8

Subjects to be covered in future volumes, all with *Canvaswork & Sail Repair*'s
step-by-step illustrated approach, include:

➢ *Sailboat Electrical Systems and Wiring*
➢ *Sailboat Diesel Engines*
➢ *Cruising Sailbat Design, Strength, and Performance*
➢ and others